Aloft at Last

How the Wright Brothers Made History

Chris Kidder

To Alan and Jeff
with hope that you will follow your dreams

ISBN 1-878405-37-3
Library of Congress Control Number 2002105565
Published by
Nags Head Art, Inc., P.O. Drawer 1809, Nags Head, NC 27959

Table of Contents

Acknowledgments

One day in early 2000, Rob Morris, my editor at *The Virginian-Pilot*, Norfolk's daily newspaper, called and asked me if I'd be interested in writing a weekly column about the Wright Brothers. "From now through the year 2003. Do you think there's enough information out there to do it?" he asked.

Neither of us knew just how much information there really was, or where my meandering research on places, people and ideas that shaped the world in which the Wrights lived and worked would take me. By the time my assignment ends, it will have been a fascinating adventure.

It wouldn't have been possible without the help of archivists at Wright State University and the Outer Banks History Center and National Park Service interpreters in Kitty Hawk and Dayton. Eminent historians Tom Crouch and Larry Tice answered questions and pointed me toward invaluable resources.

Writing a weekly column was one thing; turning those articles into a book was quite another. Without a firm kick in the seat of the pants from Steve Brumfield, I would have never gotten around to doing it. He has been my biggest fan and my trusted editor—the best brother any writer could have. Additional encouragement and a final edit came from Ronald L. Speer, a former editor at *The Virginian-Pilot*, for whom I wrote for many years. Without his keen eye and unerring sense of how words should flow, this book would have been something less than it is.

The final credit goes to Suzanne, Everett, and Mark Tate who run Nags Head Art. They followed my weekly columns in the newspaper and asked for the opportunity to publish them. They've had phenomenal success publishing Suzanne's books, but mine will be their first book not authored by Suzanne. I'm honored by their faith in me and their interest in my subject matter. (Everett, by the way, is related to Dan, Bill and Tommy Tate, Kitty Hawkers who assisted the Wrights with their flying experiments.)

Introduction

Orville and Wilbur Wright first flew an engine-powered, heavier-than-air machine at Kitty Hawk, North Carolina, on December 17, 1903. Not together, of course. On December 14, Wilbur won a coin toss to be the "operator," as the Wrights termed it, of the first attempted flight. Perhaps because he was the less dextrous of the two brothers, Wilbur's attempt failed, leaving the plane damaged. After repairs were made, Orville took his turn at the controls three days later and succeeded, flying 120 feet in 12 seconds.

Wilbur and Orville then traded turns for three more flights, the longest lasting 59 seconds and covering 852 feet but ending in a crash. Since the plane flew only a few feet off the ground, only the plane itself suffered damage.

The Wright Flyer was little more than a glider gussied up with a small engine and two propellers. There was no cockpit, no seat, nothing more than home-sewn muslin stretched over spruce to form each wing and a couple of crude controls for a man stretched out flat on his belly, one to clutch and one to operate by shifting his hips. Crude as it was, this machine built from common materials and bicycle parts proved capable of controlled, sustained flight while other more complicated, more costly machines had been abysmal failures.

Not only were the odds against such a machine, they were stacked against the operators as well. Wilbur and Orville weren't trained engineers; they didn't have the backing of their government or any other prestigious group. They were bicycle mechanics, obsessed with the idea that man could fly.

The Wrights' interest in flying "began when we were children," wrote Orville in a 1920 narrative, published later as *How We Invented the Airplane*. "Father brought home to us a small toy actuated by a rubber string which would lift itself into the air. We built a number of copies of this toy, which flew successfully."

In 1899, a book about birds rekindled their interest. "We could not understand that there was anything about a bird that would enable it to fly that could not be built on a larger scale and used by man," he wrote.

In 1900, Wilbur put their interest in other words. Writing to Octave Chanute, the leading American aviation pioneer of his day, he said, "For some years I have been afflicted with the belief that flight is possible to man. My disease has increased in severity and I feel it will soon cost me an increased amount of money if not my life. I have been trying to arrange my affairs in such a way that I can devote my entire time for a few months to experiments in this field."

And so the story began. The quest wasn't new, nor was it particularly American. Since before the time of Leonardo da Vinci in the 15th century, countless inventors had fiddled with a variety of methods and means to achieve flight. Gliders, hot air balloons and other contraptions had been launched and stayed airborne, carrying men to destinations around the globe. But successful flight had been without control; the machine and their operators were at the mercy of the winds and weather. There seemed to be no prospect for dependable travel or for warfare and commerce based on air transportation. Until the Wrights flew at Kitty Hawk, man could not fly like the birds, taking off and landing at will.

What set the Wrights apart in their quest to fly "was an extraordinary ability to analyze their experience," wrote Tom Crouch, chairman of the Department of Aeronautics at the Smithsonian Institution's National Air & Space Museum, in *The Bishop's Boys* "Both of them understood the world in terms of graphic and concrete images; more important, they could apply these observations of physical and mechanical reality to new situations. It was the very core of their shared genius."

The world the Wright brothers knew in 1900 was quite different than our world today. Dayton was a hotbed of business innovation and home to several notable eccentrics whose ranks the Wright boys would soon join. The Outer Banks was an outpost so remote that it took Wilbur three days to find a boatman in Elizabeth City willing to carry him to Kitty Hawk. Dozens of men on both sides of the Atlantic were trying very publicly to solve the problem of practical flight. These attempts and the extensive news coverage some were given–along with the Wrights' distrust of publicizing their own achievements–helped delay the recognition and reward the Wrights expected and deserved for their invention.

The family is an important part of the Wrights' success. Without the freedom to tinker and travel unencumbered by the details of day-to-day life, made possible by the devotion and service of their sister, Katharine, it is doubtful the two brothers could have accomplished what they did in so little time. And, for better or worse, the Wright patriarch, Milton, a bishop in the United Brethren Church, shaped his sons' personalities with his view of the world as a hostile and untrustworthy place. This view shaped their friendships and their business decisions throughout their lives.

But, in the end, the story comes down to one simple set of facts: Orville and Wilbur Wright accomplished in 12 seconds at Kitty Hawk what men had tried to achieve for centuries. They were successful on their own terms, armed with faith in their own abilities and in the infallibility of science, and with more than a little luck.

AUTHOR'S NOTE: Excerpts from the Wrights' letters and diaries are used in this book as they were written by the Wrights and other correspondents. Spelling, punctuation and grammar have been reproduced as they appear in the original documents.

The State of Aviation, 1900

Octave Chanute's glider

Chapter One

The wrong place at the right time

Invention is the coming together of several circumstances, the least of which is luck. Many social historians, including Jared Diamond, author of the Pulitzer Prize-winning book, *Guns, Germs, and Steel,* believe that geography and a social climate conducive to creative thinking are two of the most relevant factors determining the why and where of mankind's most notable innovations.

As Diamond points out in his book, technological innovation in weapons and transportation played crucial roles in the development of the world as we know it today.

Heavier-than-air flight promised revolutionary advances on both counts. And by the mid-19th century all the major European powers —heavily populated by the day's standards and desperately jockeying for colonial territory around the globe—were at the brink of breaking the bonds that tied men to the ground.

There's no question Europe had the incentives and a distinct edge in the race to fly. Europeans had already conquered lighter-than-air flight and their governments and private foundations had been encouraging inventors to create a heavier-than-air machine that would actually fly. Hundreds of them had given the task their best shot, to no avail.

China and Japan, both formidable civilizations within their own spheres of influence, had been flying kites for centuries. Chinese kites achieved perfect equilibrium—the pivotal problem with most early air-plane designs—through flexibility. In his 1894 book, *Progress in Flying Machines,* Octave Chanute predicted, "It would not at all be surprising to find, should a stable aeroplane be hereafter produced, that it has its pro-totype in a Chinese kite." The Japanese built and flew mammoth kites from tethers, some weighing as much as 1,700 pounds with 50-foot wingspans. But neither country showed an interest in launching men into the air.

In 1884, a Russian, Alexander Mozhaiski, built a steam-powered monoplane that flew 100 feet before crashing near St. Petersburg. It was the second documented power-assisted take-off in history, but the attempt appears to have contributed nothing to Western efforts to fly. The Russians weren't heard from again in aviation circles until the early 1900s.

But at that point the Russians were ahead of the Americans. Patent records before 1890 show a distinct lack of interest in flight on the part of American inventors. It wasn't until after that date that American engineers began seriously confronting the challenge to fly. Much, if not all, of their theoretical knowledge came from Europe.

The United States lacked organized support for aviation invention. Although the Smithsonian Institution was involved with Samuel Langley's flying experiments and acted as an informal clearinghouse for aviation information, there were only one or two American associations devoted to advancing aviation. Most European countries had a well established network of institutions devoted to aeronautical ventures.

Unlike Europe, the United States had fewer reasons to be interested in aviation. It had no major colonial interests abroad and did not feel vulnerable militarily. There was no strong government support for developing an airplane.

On the home front, the transcontinental railroad, considered a modern marvel, had just been completed in 1869. The automobile, introduced in Europe about that same time, promised individual freedom to travel farther and faster than ever before. America's creative minds had plenty of more-needed opportunities for invention.

Early automobile
Lib. of Cong., Prints & Photos Div.
LC-DIG-pprs-4a18078r

It's often said that necessity is the mother of invention. In Diamond's view, many inventions—including the Wrights' airplane in the context of America's need for that technology in 1900—are the mother of necessity. Once heavier-than-air flight had been achieved, and the Wrights had developed a plane that could be manufactured, they had a difficult time convincing people to buy it.

Given all that, it seemed hardly likely two brothers from Dayton, Ohio, on their own, without private or public financial support or patronage, would solve a problem that had been stumping creative thinkers worldwide for centuries.

Chapter Two

Flapping wings and other ideas that didn't fly

When Orville and Wilbur Wright began their quest to fly, the idea that man might soar like birds was nothing new. From early Greek mythology through the Renaissance, right up to the Wright brothers' historic first flights at Kitty Hawk in 1903, hundreds of men had attempted heavier-than-air, powered flight.

Octave Chanute, a French-born American, capped an illustrious engineering career as a champion of flight. In the early 1890s, at a time when most Victorians believed man's place was firmly on the ground where God put him, Chanute documented aviation history in *Progress in Flying Machines*. He did not believe flight should be left to creatures born with wings. And, as an astute observer of invention, he believed that powered flight was not only possible but imminent.

As the Victorian era ended, public opinion began to change. For the first time in history, a cross-section of scientists, engineers, inventors, scholars, politicians and the general populace throughout the Western world began to publicly share the same belief. The possibility of powered flight became a popular topic of conversation. Newspapers around the world reported the latest attempts at flight and, with more than a little smugness, the failures. Books about the theories of flight and man's attempts to conquer the air, including Chanute's, had been published and were widely read.

Empire of the Air, a book about the flight of birds published in 1881, was written by Louis-Pierre Mouillard. Mouillard, a French poet and champion of manned flight who died in 1897, inspired Chanute and, later, Wilbur Wright. Richard Rathbun, assistant to Samuel Pierpont Langley, secretary of the Smithsonian Institution, sent Wilbur a reprint from Mouillard's book, along with several other articles, in 1899.

Writing for the Aero Club of America *Bulletin* in 1912, Wilbur called Mouillard's book "one of the most remarkable pieces of aeronautical literature that has ever been published. . . . His observations upon the habits

Besnier, a French locksmith, invented this unsuccessful flying contraption in 1678.

of vultures led him to the conclusion that flight without motors was possible to man, and this idea he presented to his readers with an enthusiasm so inspiring and convincing that his book produced results of the greatest importance in the history of flight."

"There is no doubt," Wilbur continued, "that the reading of this book was one of the main factors in inducing Mr. Chanute to undertake his experiments, and I know it was one of the inspiring causes of the efforts of the Wright brothers."

"With the possible exception of Lilienthal, none of the men who wrote on aviation in the 19th century possessed such power to draw recruits to a belief in the possibility of motorless human flight."

Mouillard, said Wilbur, was "one of the greatest missionaries of the flying cause."

The 18th and 19th centuries had been years of mechanical invention. Hot air balloons, successfully launched and flown in the late 1700s, were followed by steerable airships (dirigibles) and gliders less than 100 years later.

But with the rapid evolution of mechanically-powered transportation on the ground, the push to put that technology to work in the air took on new urgency. Realizing that profit, prestige and political advantage would be the ultimate rewards, governments, scientific academies and private investors poured money into inventing a maneuverable, self-powered machine that could provide dependable transportation above the ground.

But for all the years of trial-and-error, for all the effort and money, in two centuries, little real progress in heavier-than-air flight had been made. Men had invented all sorts of contraptions, and some had actually made it into the air. But no one had figured out how to reliably launch a powered craft and control it once it was airborne.

Looking back through Chanute's book at the drawings of pre-Wright airplanes, it becomes clear that failure didn't stem from a lack of creativity. Inventors took their cues from birds, fish and fanciful flights of imagination that resulted in an amazing assortment of machines.

Many of the efforts assumed that man, like birds, would fly by flapping wings. Some machines, like the wood apparatus invented by a French locksmith named Besnier in 1678 with four wings measuring about 2 by 3 feet each attached to long poles and tied to a man's wrists and ankles, were relatively portable and simple. Others, like a parachute-style winged machine built by another Frenchman, Louis-Charles Letur in 1852, were as big as a house.

Although most attempts with flapping wings relied on human muscle-power for propulsion, as early as 1784 inventors were considering the use of some sort of motor. F. D. Artingstall, an Englishman, drew plans for an aerial locomotive in the mid-1800's, using a lightweight steam engine to power wings that opened and closed like pairs of Venetian blinds.

According to Chanute, "When steam was turned on, the wings worked vigorously, but the machine jerked up and down, rushed from side to side, and, in fact, performed all kinds of gymnastic movements except flight."

In 1890, E. P. Frost presented plans to the British Aeronautical Society for a 650-pound steam-bird machine with a 30 foot wing span. The machine never flew, of course.

At the same society meeting, another would-be flier, H. Middleton, exhibited two smaller bird-like flying machines. It can be assumed that because they broke many of the laws of aerodynamics, they weren't successful fliers either.

Chapter Three

America had its share of impractical dreamers

Americans, for the most part, eschewed flapping wings but offered their share of crackpot ideas. In 1890, in a letter published in the *New York Herald*, John Holland claimed to have invented a 7,000-pound, steam-driven, marine screw-propelled craft. It could stay aloft for up to 84 hours, he said, but he couldn't disclose the design details until he'd secured a patent.

In his book, *The Bishop's Boys*, aviation historian Tom Crouch related numerous accounts: In 1896 Capt. John Veiru "unveiled plans for a fish-shaped, paddle wheel flying machine; Victor Oches, a convict serving time in a New York jail, offered a $25,000 craft he claimed capable of flying at 3,400 mph; At about the same time, the Rev. B. Cannon of Pittsburg, Texas, made public his Ezekiel Flying Machine, an invention which took its design cues from biblical descriptions."

One of America's more notable failures at flight was a Carolina boy born about 100 miles from Kitty Hawk. James Henry Gatling was born to Jordan and Mary Barnes Gatling in 1816, in a small log cabin in Maney's Neck, North Carolina, near Murfreesboro. When James Henry was still a small child, his father amassed more than 1,200 acres, and the family moved into a great house more befitting one of the state's largest landowners.

One of six children, James Henry and his brothers attended Buckhorn Academy, where they were taught the classics. At home, they were taught to tinker with machinery. During their childhood, Jordan invented and patented a cotton seed planter and other farm equipment.

Of the Gatling boys, it seems that Richard, James Henry's younger brother, had the earmarks of genius and the knack for successful invention. Richard finished school at 15, worked at a variety of jobs for a few years and continued his tinkering. He improved his father's planting machine, adapting it for rice, to get his first patent. He then moved to St.

Louis, invented a wheat-planting machine and made a small fortune.

A few years later, he earned a medical degree but returned to inventing agricultural machinery until the Civil War began in 1861. He then put his creative energies into producing a gun that would revolutionize warfare. The first version of his machine battery gun, popularly known as the "Gatling gun," was finished in 1862 but not adopted by the U.S. government until after the war's end.

Through the years, Richard pursued a number of interests and achieved international fame. Had he tackled the problem of flight, history might have been quite different. But it was James Henry who took up the quest.

Evidence suggests James Henry tackled his quest to fly in highly creative ways. He grew up jumping from barn lofts with umbrellas and wearing wings made of corn shucks. He then devoted years to building model airplanes, reported historian Stephen Kirk, who chronicled the Wrights' achievement in *First in Flight*. But he relied on his imagination, without any scientific investigation into the known principles of flight or propulsion.

By 1865 James Henry was ready to build a full-scale model. His plans were thwarted when robbers ransacked the family plantation and stole the $1,700 he had saved for the project.

Seven years later, he tried again. This time, he built a twin-engine machine that bystanders called "Old Turkey Buzzard." Most historians believe the machine was launched from the roof of his cotton gin and crashed on its first attempted flight in 1873. Kirk says Gatling never tried to fly again.

But around Murfreesboro many folks have insisted James Henry did fly. Several reports from eyewitnesses have been published in local history books. They claim they saw James Henry soaring over his cotton fields 25 years before the Wright brothers flew at Kitty Hawk.

It's ironic that most other American attempts at powered flight before the 1890s used screw-type propellers not unlike one perfected by Richard Gatling. Several of these contraptions were patented in the last half of the 19th century, but none ever flew.

Chapter Four

Other inventors laid the foundation

Orville and Wilbur Wright would never have solved the secret of heavier-than-air, powered flight and flown at Kitty Hawk in 1903 without the well-publicized failures of other would-be aviators. Although man had always considered the possibility of flight, only in the Wrights' lifetime had the fantasy edged close to reality.

Dr. George A. Spratt of Pennsylvania was a contemporary of the Wright brothers. Like them, he had been fascinated by flight most of his life, and he sought the advice of Octave Chanute.

Unlike the Wrights, Spratt favored flying machines with a pivot wing, rather than fixed wing, design. He shared this preference with Chanute. Although some aviation historians credit Spratt with persuading Chanute pivot wings were better, it appears Chanute was already working on the idea of "automatic control" and "oscillating wings" before the two men met. Neither man had any luck convincing the Wrights to use the pivot-wing design.

Chanute went so far as to hire Edward Chalmers Huffaker, a former assistant to Smithsonian Secretary and aeronautic engineer Samuel Langley, to build and test an oscillating wing glider at Kitty Hawk in 1901. He hoped the tests would interest the Wrights in using his design. Instead, Chanute's glider only convinced the brothers that the design had little merit.

Huffaker, a graduate of Emory and Henry College and the University of Virginia, where he earned an M.S. in physics, began building gliders in 1892. He authored a pamphlet on flying, *On Soaring Flight*, recommended to Wilbur Wright by the Smithsonian Institution in 1899. According to Crouch, by 1901 Huffaker was considered one of the "best educated aeronautical experimenters in the United States." His actual hands-on experience with full-scale flying machines, however, was limited.

Chanute had mentored Huffaker for over 10 years before hiring him to work with the Wrights, but the younger man was far from deferential. He changed Chanute's design and constructed the wing struts of the glider out of cardboard tubing. He also experimented with a novel method of attaching the wing fabric.

Chanute visited Huffaker at his home in Chuckey City, Tennessee, to look over the glider. He was dismayed by the changes. "The mechanical details and connections of the gliding machine . . . are so weak, that I fear they will not stand long enough to test the efficiency of the ideas in its design . . . ," Chanute wrote to Wilbur Wright in late June, 1901.

Huffaker arrived at the Wright brothers' camp in Kitty Hawk on July 18. According to Crouch, his glider performed so poorly that he abandoned it. Other historians reported the glider was ruined by rain before it could be flown. In either case, by the time Chanute arrived on August 1, the glider was beyond repair and Huffaker had lost interest in it.

Huffaker was "brimming over with enthusiasm for the Wrights and their glider," wrote Crouch. "He is astonished at our mechanical facility," Wilbur noted in a letter to his father, "and, as he attributes his own failures to the lack of this, he thinks the problem solved when these difficulties are overcome, while we expect to find further difficulties of a theoretical nature which must be met by new mechanical designs."

Huffaker was smart enough to recognize the Wrights hadn't learned everything there was to know about the physics of flying. He and Spratt both pointed out that the center of pressure on a wing reversed as it traveled through the air. But Huffaker remained unconcerned about the fixed wing's tendency to stall, even after witnessing the Wrights' glider stalling several times.

Although the Wrights disliked Huffaker personally, he had standing in the aeronautical community. His support of their wing design over Chanute's must have encouraged their refusal to consider changing their approach.

Spratt, realizing the shortcomings of Huffaker's 1901 glider were in the construction, not the design, was not swayed. He and Chanute continued to support pivoting wings even after the Wrights flew successfully in a fixed-wing plane.

After working with the Wrights at Kitty Hawk, Spratt spent the next 30 years designing pivot-wing gliders and airplanes on his own. He built and flew his first powered pivot-wing airplane in 1912. Spratt's son, George G., followed his father into aviation and achieved considerable success with his patented "ControlWing" design.

In one of the few published criticisms of the Wrights' engineering ability, George G. defended his father's preference for the stall-proof, pivot-wing design. The Wrights' decision to use fixed-wing technology "has probably cost more lives than any other [decision] made in aircraft history," said George, although that assessment would not be shared by every aeronautical engineer.

Chapter Five

U.S. government backed the wrong plane

Orville and Wilbur Wright worked through the winter of 1901-1902, testing wind foils and trying to get a better grasp on the aerodynamics of flight. Their glider experiments at Kitty Hawk in the summer of 1901 had been, in Wilbur's view, a disaster.

They had based their expectations on existing science, and it let them down. Wilbur, a most meticulous man, wasn't going to let that happen again. He double-checked accepted theories and made his own calculations from then on.

Octave Chanute believed the Wrights to be closest to solving the problems of heavier-than-air flight, but few people knew of their experiments. Although Wilbur had reluctantly addressed the Society of Western Engineers in Chicago in September 1901, he had been purposefully vague. He had no desire for public scrutiny at this point in his quest to fly.

Because the Wrights deliberately avoided publicity, few Americans outside a circle of Chanute and his fellow engineers, had ever heard of the two brothers from Dayton. Most, if asked, would have said that Samuel P. Langley, esteemed Secretary of the Smithsonian Institution in Washington, D.C. was America's leading aeronaut. If anyone was taking bets on who would build the first successful flying machine, the odds would have run in Langley's favor.

The Wrights, like Chanute and the German aviator Otto Lilienthal, believed the future of human flight was in gliders. The goal of some early aviators was merely controlled gliding. If man could mimic the birds, they reasoned, he would have achieved enough. Orville and Wilbur could see beyond gliders, but they believed they had to first learn the secrets of controlling motorless flight before powered flight could be successful. Many of their better-known contemporaries, including Langley, disagreed—and failed.

The Wright brothers thought Langley's methodology was wrong and found his data in *Experiments in Aerodynamics* faulty. In an article written in 1908 for *Century* magazine, Orville said, "Yet a critical examination of the data upon which [Langley] based his conclusions as to the pressure at small angles shows results so various as to make many of his conclusions little better than guess-work."

But the American government believed Langley would be successful, and in 1898 the Board of Ordnance and Fortification of the War Department allotted $50,000 for his Aerodrome project.

By the time the Wrights were refining the science of flight in 1901, Langley was a year-and-a-half behind on his promise to develop, construct and test a manned version of his flying machine. Although he attempted to keep the details and progress of his government contract under wraps, keeping such secrets in Washington were difficult. Considering who Langley was and what he had already accomplished, secrecy was impossible.

Langley, a contemporary of Chanute's, was born and educated in Boston. Typical of most men working as engineers and scientists at the turn of the century, he was largely self-educated in those fields. Nevertheless, he had an illustrious career in astronomy, physics and mathematics. He worked at the Harvard and Allegheny observatories and the U.S. Naval Academy before joining the Smithsonian.

During his tenure at the Smithsonian, from 1887 until his death in 1906, Langley enjoyed a position of power and privilege. According to Phil Scott in *The Shoulders of Giants*, after his appointment as Secretary of the Smithsonian, he "counted among his new friends in Washington the nation's most famous men."

In spite of Langley's prominence, when he published his conclusion that mechanical flight was theoretically possible in *Experiments in Aerodynamics* in 1891, his peers were skeptical of his claims. In defense of his book, he drew upon the resources of the Smithsonian and, according to Scott, began assembling "a team of the country's most talented engineers and machinists, with the goal of producing a powered model capable of sustained flight." The flights of his steam-powered model Aerodromes in 1896 were successful.

The first model, weighing 26 pounds and traveling at a top speed of

25 mph with a 1 horsepower engine, flew about 3,300 feet. The flight was witnessed and photographed by the great American inventor Alexander Graham Bell, who publicly proclaimed the flight a remarkable success.

A few months later, Langley launched a second Aerodrome over the

Potomac River (none of Langley's Aerodromes were capable of taking off under their own power; all had to be catapulted from a rail). This machine flew for three-quarters of a mile reaching an air speed of 30 mph. These were the first heavier-than-air flights ever documented.

The final attempt to launch Samuel Langley's Aerodrome was made just days before the Wrights flew in 1903.

Langley believed his models proved that powered flight could be achieved and had no plans to build a full-sized plane. But skeptics, once again, made him feel compelled to pursue his work to its logical conclusion.

But Langley, like most of the successful model airplane builders before him, did not have a firm grasp of aerodynamic principles. As the size of an aircraft grows, the requirements for some elements of its design change exponentially. It is not possible to simply make every part four times or ten times larger and fly. Not only did Langley err in ignoring the interrelationships between each element of his plane, but also he relied on mathematical equations and calculations that later proved to be wrong.

In 1903, years behind schedule and $23,000 over his government-allotted budget, Langley launched his full-sized, manned Aerodrome from the top of a houseboat on the Potomac. The huge machine was as large as the house. Two sets of tandem wings each measured 11 x 48 feet; the water-cooled, 52 horsepower engine weighed 200 pounds; the lifting surfaces equaled more than 1,000 square feet.

The Aerodrome was launched unsuccessfully in October. Charles Manley, the pilot, told the press it was improperly balanced. A second try in December produced similar results: The machine flew off the end of the catapult device mounted on the houseboat and promptly sank in the river.

Chapter Six

Wrights were inspired by German flier

Otto Lilienthal was a Prussian German born in 1848, some 20 years before the Wrights. He became interested in the idea of mechanical flight

Otto Lilienthal

as a child. In his early teens, he and his brother built flying contraptions and attempted flight by running down hillsides flapping homemade wings. Leaving these childish attempts behind, Lilienthal graduated from the Berlin Trade Academy and made a comfortable living manufacturing steam boilers. He was able to earn the means and time to indulge his passion for flight.

After studying the work of a contemporary, Louis-Pierre Mouillard, and Sir George Cayley (1773-1857), Lilienthal spent years systematically studying the flight of birds, eventually narrowing his focus to wings and principles of lift. Over five years in the mid-1890s, he built 18 different monoplane and biplane gliders and took part in more than 2,000 glider flights.

No one had succeeded with powered flight, Lilienthal later wrote, because "our physical and technical knowledge and our practical experience were by far insufficient to overcome a mechanical task of such magnitude without more preliminaries."

When the Wrights began studying the problem of powered flight, they agreed with Lilienthal's assessment. Men needed to understand how machines moved through the air and how to control those movements before they began attaching motors to wings. And, while most of their contemporaries chose to ignore this caveat, the Wrights followed in Lilienthal's footsteps.

In 1889, Lilienthal published a book translated into English as

Birdflight as the Basis of Aviation. The book proposed that arched or vaulted wings were necessary for controlled flight and included tables of calculations showing how much wind was needed to lift wings of certain sizes and shapes.

In 1891, Lilienthal began years of gliding experiments in which he launched himself into the air—unlike Langley, Chanute and other aviation pioneers of his day who were content to watch while hired hands took the risk of breaking their necks. Lilienthal made good copy and his exploits were published by newspapers around the world. In Dayton, the Wrights followed his progress and admired his methodology.

By mid-1896, Lilienthal had flown in 16 different gliders, according to Crouch. He used monoplanes, biplanes and bat-like creations whose wings were built of split willow and bamboo covered with cotton twill. On August 9 of that year, he launched himself from a hill in a monoplane glider and promptly crashed, broke his spine and died.

Wilbur read about Lilienthal's death in a news wire report that came across a teletype machine the brothers kept in their bicycle shop on Williams Street in West Dayton. (The brothers had previously published a newspaper and invested in a teletype machine. The newspaper folded, but they kept the teletype.)

Wilbur later said his ". . . active interest in aeronautical problems dates back to the death of Lilienthal. . . . The brief notice of his death which appeared in the telegraphic news at that time aroused a passive interest which had existed from my childhood. . . ."

By the time the Wrights began building their first glider in 1899, Lilienthal's lift calculations were accepted as accurate by everyone who was anyone in aviation. Langley and Chanute, the two leading American aeronautical experts, based their design and performance expectations on Lilienthal's data.

"We had studied Lilienthal's tables of figures with awe," said Orville in an interview with *Boy's Life* magazine in 1914. They would later find the tables were incorrect, but it never dulled their admiration for Lilienthal's accomplishments.

Chapter Seven

French offered inspiration and challenge

One of the most serious challenges to the Wright brothers' claim to first flight came from France.

The French were keen on solving the problems of powered flight and had been working on it longer than their American counterparts. Before 1900, the French Society of Physics, Academy of Sciences, French Aeronautical Society and the 1887 Scientific Congress at Toulouse all spent time and funds evaluating and encouraging several would-be aviators.

The French were so intrigued by the possibility of flying that anyone in Europe who had visions of constructing a successful flying machine eventually made his way to Paris to demonstrate his ideas. Crowds would gather, scientists would pore over plans and prospectus, but it all came to naught.

It should be noted that the French did invent the first successful, steerable airship, or dirigible, in 1884. But an airship wasn't an airplane, and it was the maneuverability and bird-like freedom that an airplane promised that held the public's fancy.

In the late 1700s, two Frenchmen had introduced a small-scale flapping, flying machine to the French Academy of Sciences. Less than 100 years later, Alphonse Pénaud improved on the design and a copy of his rubber-band-powered "toy" landed in the hands of young Orville and Wilbur Wright. Many elements of Pénaud's design were used by Samuel Langley.

But before Langley joined the race to fly, two other Frenchmen, Hureau deVilleneuve and M. Jobert, were taking Pénaud's ideas further. They fully believed the first successful airplane would be built like birds with flapping wings, and in the 1870s, they were peppering the French scientific community with models and requests for funds to support their dreams.

Felix du Temple, a French naval officer, patented a boat-like flying machine in 1857 although it never flew. Gustave Trouvé was another Frenchman with high-flying ideas. His work was serious enough to be discussed at length by Chanute in *Progress in Flying Machines*, but, in the end, was no more successful than any of the others except Clement Ader.

Clément Ader was one exception. Born on February 4, 1841 in Muret, France, he was a self-taught engineer and dabbled in a variety of fields outside aviation like most inventors and flying enthusiasts of his day. He worked for several years as an engineer with the French Administration of Bridges and Highways but quit to pursue his other interests.

Aside from his airplanes, his most notable invention was a microphone which allowed the stereophonic transmission of sound. In 1881, he transmitted a musical performance in stereo via telephone from the Paris Opera to the International Electrical Exhibition some distance away.

Ader's biggest claim to fame, however, came from his interest in aviation. In 1870, at his own expense, he built a hot air balloon for the French to use in the Franco-German War.

By 1890, he had designed and built a steam-powered, bat-winged monoplane—*l'Eole*—driven by a propeller, which lifted a few inches off the ground under its own power and flew about 160 feet before it crashed. The machine proved incapable of sustained flight or of being controlled. Although the short trip didn't qualify as true flight, he was the first to prove that a powered aircraft could, indeed, launch itself into the air from level ground.

After the promising performance of *l'Eole*, the French military took an interest in Ader's work and the government bankrolled a new flying machine, the *Avion*. (Ader is credited with inventing the French word avion, meaning aircraft, as an acronym for "*Apparieil Volant Imitant les Oisaux Naturels*," roughly translated "flying machines imitating natural birds.")

It is believed that Ader built two versions of the *Avion* but only the second was completed. *Avion III*, a great bat-like, folding-winged machine with dual propellers driven by a 40-horsepower steam engine, was finished in 1897.

Tests of *Avion III* by Ader and the French government were held at a military airfield near Paris in late fall of that year. They were witnessed only by some members of the military and a commission of military and engineering experts appointed by the Minister of War.

Although no official announcement was made about *Avion's* field performance, the government withdrew monetary support for the project and Ader never built another flying machine. But a few years after the Wright brothers flew at Kitty Hawk, the French claimed the Wrights were stealing Ader's place in aviation history.

Frenchman Clément Ader's l'Eole *is pictured in this fanciful etching.*

Chapter Eight

British efforts to fly had serious backing

The British at the height of their empire under Queen Victoria weren't about to be left behind. Like the French, they had an active aeronautical society which served as a sounding board—and, occasionally, as a financial backer—for various flying schemes. The Aeronautical Society of Great Britain, founded in 1866, spent its first 40 years evaluating a remarkable variety of flying inventions.

Soon after the society was formed, Mr. F. D. Artingstall informed the group of his experiments with steam-driven flapping wings. He attached his wings to a lightweight locomotive engine with pistons, allowing the wings to open and close like Venetian blinds. In *Progress in Flying Machines*, Chanute reported that Artingstall gave up his experiments after two engines exploded.

In 1868, I. Palmer exhibited a pair of powered wings on a rotating axle to the society. Chanute described the motion of this machine "like the action of a duck's foot in swimming." Palmer never did anything further with his invention.

At the same meeting, I. M. Kaufmann, an engineer from Glasgow, unveiled another set of steam-powered wings. As soon as Kaufmann's 42-pound scale model powered up and furiously flapped a few times, the wings broke off. His design would have weighed 7,000 or 8,000 pounds at full size. "It may well be doubted whether this would have proved effective," noted Chanute.

R. C. Jay came before the society twice in the 1870s with oscillating-wing models. He claimed the multiple wing movements would support a machine in air in the same fashion figure eight hand movements support a body treading water.

Charles Spencer, a small, athletic, 140-pound man, exhibited a man-powered machine that exceeded 110 feet in length. With running starts, he was able to propel the machine into the air for 120 to 130 feet. Chanute expressed doubt that most men could accomplish such a feat. W.

Quartermain, weighing in over 200 pounds, designed a machine patterned after the stag beetle, with four wings, but was unable to lift himself—and the 135-pound machine—off the ground.

In 1890, the society examined a photograph of a 650-pound machine created by E. P. Frost. Frost's steam-powered bird had a 30-foot wing span designed to look and work like the wings of a crow. At the same meeting, two additional bird designs were submitted by Mr. H. Middleton. None of the machines worked.

All of these inventors ignored the work of their countryman William Matthew Henson, who in 1842 patented an aeroplane with fixed-wing surfaces. The design called for canvas or oiled silk to be stretched over a trussed frame. The machine had a horizontal tail and a rudder. Henson never built a full-sized aircraft, however, and left England for America in the early 1840s.

No one knows what might have happened had he persevered. According to Chanute, "His general design evidences careful thought and possesses some excellent features." In fact, later aviation historians would note the similarities between Henson's design and planes used by the military during World War I.

But Henson's work was not completely original. He drew heavily upon the experience and theories of Sir George Cayley. Cayley, an English baronet, was a scholar and careful experimenter. In 1799, at the age of 24, he began designing fixed-wing aircraft to gain knowledge of the principles of aviation.

Cayley built the first successful glider in 1804. Although it took him until 1853 to build one that would successfully carry a man into the air, he was the first to do so.

As in other countries, some British inventors skipped gliding and went straight to building powered machines. Sir Hiram Stevens Maxim belonged to this group.

Maxim was born into an American fam-

Sir George Cayley

ily that made its name in the munitions business. He took the family business to England where he spent a few years fascinated by the idea of inventing the perfect propulsion system to launch a man into flight. He later went on to have several successful inventions, including a particularly deadly machine gun, for which he was knighted.

"Engineers and scientists have long admitted that a flying machine would be possible provided that some one should succeed in producing a motive power sufficiently light and strong," he wrote not long after he began studying the problems of flight in 1889. He believed it was a problem he could solve.

Just as Chanute had done—and as Wilbur Wright would do—Maxim studied what progress had already been made in flying machines.

"It is true that a great many experiments in this line had been conducted by others, but generally on an exceedingly small scale, with very imperfect apparatus, and the results had always been most unsatisfactory," he explained in the January 1895 edition of *Century* magazine. "I therefore determined to make my experiments on a scale sufficiently large to render them of some value."

By 1891, Maxim had run preliminary experiments. "The results seemed to show that unless there should be some unfavorable factor relating wholly to size, it would be possible to make a practical flying machine," he wrote.

In 1893, according to author Fred Howard in *Wilbur and Orville*, after working on a full-sized aircraft for a year, Maxim told reporters "propulsion and lifting are solved problems. The rest is a mere matter of time."

"Time ran out for Maxim on July 31, 1894," wrote Howard, "when his unbird-like creation lumbered down an 1,800-foot track on its cast-iron wheels and struggled 2 feet into the air before its upward progress was arrested."

Maxim had spent nearly $100,000 of his own money to design and test his lightweight, steam-powered, 160-horsepower engine. Unfortunately, he put two of the engines in a gigantic, 4-ton biplane that had little else to recommend it in the way of practical controls. The 200-

foot-long biplane sported dual 18-foot propellers and a 107-foot wingspan, designed to carry a crew of three men. After its crash, Maxim lost interest in the project and never attempted flight again.

Peter Jakab and Rick Young, editors of *The Published Writings of Wilbur and Orville Wright,* summed up Maxim's achievement: "Maxim had shown that with enough power, a winged aircraft could indeed be coaxed into the air."

Maxim's failure, according to Wilbur Wright, several years after his own successful flights, was that he'd become convinced effective propulsion was the key to flight. "The problem of stability, which had caused [Langley, Lilienthal, Maxim, Chanute and Ader] to drop the problem, was yet seemingly untouched, so far as a practical solution was concerned."

The Wright Family

The Wrights' Hawthorn Street home in Dayton, Ohio
Lib. of Cong., Prints & Photos Div. LC-DIG-pprs-00523v

Chapter Nine

Childhood years

Orville and Wilbur Wright believed, like the boys in Horatio Alger's popular stories of their youth, that hard work and faith in themselves would ensure success. They were quintessential American entrepreneurs, and yet they remained boys in many ways. They pursued dreams of flight inspired by the books and toys of childhood. Their foibles, as well as their combined genius, were the product of growing up in a family both typical of its time and uniquely eccentric. Who the two brothers were as children is what they became as adults. And in spite of the fame they eventually achieved, they never left home.

It was common for men of the 1800s to be competent in a variety of trades from an early age and the Wrights were no exception. They were decent carpenters and mechanics; they built and ran printing presses and a variety of other gadgets and machines. They also knew how to sew and cook.

Although neither got his high school diploma or attended college, the brothers were voracious readers of Dayton's many newspapers and the scientific books in the family's extensive library. "We were lucky enough to grow up in a home environment where there was always much encouragement to children to pursue intellectual interests; to investigate wherever aroused curiosity," Orville told biographer Fred Kelly.

The Wright brothers' parents, Milton and Susan Wright, were two Midwesterners who married relatively late in life. They were both college educated. Susan was a homemaker and died before all her children were grown. Milton was an ordained minister with the Church of the United Brethren in Christ, but he also did short stints as a school teacher and farmer. During most of Wilbur and Orville's youth, Milton served his church as a regional bishop and as editor of a series of religious newspapers.

Milton and Susan had seven children: Reuchlin, Lorin, Wilbur, Orville and Katharine; twins Otis and Ida, died shortly after birth. Wilbur was "in every sense the middle child," noted biographer Tom Crouch in *The Bishop's Boys*. He was just over four years younger than Lorin and four years older than Orville.

The family moved several times after Wilbur was born near Millville, Indiana, in 1867. In 1868, the Wrights lived in Hartsville, Indiana. In 1869, they moved to Dayton and lived in two different places before buying the house on Hawthorn Street where Orville was born in 1871. Katharine was born in the Hawthorn Street house three years later. In 1878, the family moved to Cedar Rapids, Iowa, and then, in 1880, to nearby Adair. In 1881, they moved to Henry County, Indiana. In 1884, the Wrights were back in Dayton.

The Wrights were not wealthy, but Milton earned enough money to live comfortably and own several pieces of property. He owned farms in Grant County and Millville, Indiana, and Adair, Iowa. When the family left Dayton in 1878, he was able to rent out the house on Hawthorn Street and buy a new home in Iowa. When the family moved back to Dayton, they moved into the Hawthorn Street house (after the tenants' lease expired) and stayed there until 1914.

Milton's wife, Susan, was never healthy. She suffered from rheumatism, malaria and other illnesses as a young woman. Marrying at 28, she bore seven children between 1861 and 1874. She died of tuberculosis in 1889, at the age of 58, when her youngest child, Katharine, was only 15. Susan was an invalid for most of the last six years of her life and the task of nursing fell to Wilbur, the oldest of her children still living at home.

In spite of her illness, Susan is credited with teaching her children the skills to be self-sufficient. Descended from a long line of craftsmen and carriage builders, she shared her own interests in carpentry and mechanics with them. If such skills are inherited, Wilbur and Orville could thank Susan for their abilities. Milton, it seems, had neither the inclination or time for such things.

By all accounts, the Wright children were raised with affection and a strong sense of family pride and responsibility. Although Reuchlin eventually distanced himself from his father and siblings, the others remained very close throughout most of their lives.

Chapter Ten

The Bishop

Even though Orville and Wilbur were nurtured as children and successful as adults, their lives were marked by considerable turmoil. When it comes to the brothers' inability to sustain personal relationships outside the family or get along with the world at large, most biographers draw a straight line to Milton.

For most of his adult life, Milton Wright was employed by the Church of the United Brethren in Christ. His career took the family from Indiana to Ohio, Iowa and back to Ohio—moves that don't seem unusual in this day but were far less common in the 1800s. Once the family finally settled in Dayton, his duties as bishop and editor of the *Religious Telescope* kept him traveling.

Through most of the last quarter of the 1800s, Milton was embroiled in an ideological fight within the church. He was leader and spokesman for the Radicals, a conservative faction who denounced membership in the Masonic Lodge and other secret societies and fought against modernization of the church structure.

Milton was also the church's supervisor of litigations, a difficult position for someone preaching brotherly love, but a necessary one due to a schism that left members haggling over the organization's considerable assets. Once the factions split in 1889, years of lawsuits followed as both sides tried to secure their financial legacy. He spent much of his time concerned with secular matters rather than those of a spiritual nature. That may explain why none of the three children with whom he lived ever participated in organized religion. It appears, too, that for all his influence in their lives, religion was one area where he wielded none.

Milton's home was both his office and his castle. Although he was progressive in some ways (insisting that all his children—including Katharine, the only living daughter—have the opportunity for a college education and supporting, if not encouraging, his children's risky ventures), he took his role as head of the household to the conservative extreme, demanding the patronage of his children and micro-managing their lives, even in absentia.

In spite of his dogmatic views and use of litigation, church historians and Wright biographers have judged Milton to be remarkably fair. Nevertheless, he was a man who saw things as either right or wrong: he allowed for no shades of gray in either his own actions or in his expectations of others.

It is impossible to know if Wilbur was simply doing the middle child shuffle and adapting to his father's expectations or if he was, indeed, the child most after Milton's own heart. In either case, he showed an early talent for writing, a logical approach to problem-solving and shared Milton's strong sense of justice. By the time Wilbur was in high school, Milton had pressed him into church service writing and distributing church literature in support of Radical causes.

Wilbur continued to help Milton during the years he ran the bicycle business with Orville and up until the time of his death in 1912. He attended church meetings and court hearings, took notes and wrote position papers. It appears Wilbur enjoyed wading into the fray on his father's behalf. Even when his own plate was full with lawsuits protecting the Wright Flyer patents, he continued to perform these services out of devotion to Milton, not the church.

The two oldest Wright boys married, but none of the bishop's three youngest children showed any inclination to leave the family nest until Katharine married, at the age of 52, just two years before she died. The bishop lived 28 years in relatively good health after Susan died, but never considered remarrying. Although he was largely an absentee husband, it appears that he was very devoted to Susan. In 1901, he was still counting the years since her death. She was, he wrote, the "light of my home."

The bishop was a central figure in his children's lives, and even as adults, they remained mindful of how their father expected them to think and act. Wilbur and Orville were life-long teetotalers. Neither smoked nor swore. Their insistence on formal dress even when working under extreme weather conditions and their rule of not working on Sunday were often impractical restrictions and best explained by Milton's influence.

The three kept in frequent contact with one another when traveling, sharing the day-to-day details of their lives, often with humor, but seldom delving into deeper issues or philosophical discussion.

Milton's negative view of human nature was his most unfortunate influence on his children. His boys were unreasonably suspicious of others' motives. "They took up the challenge of selling the airplane with the memory of their father's church struggles fresh in their minds," wrote Crouch. Adhering to their father's mantra to trust no one but family, they refused most advice given by Octave Chanute regarding patents and the marketing of their airplane, even though Chanute had more business experience and better connections with those interested in purchasing aircraft. They turned down offers of collaboration from Glenn Curtiss, Augustus Herring and others to keep from sharing any details of their own work—and often found themselves competing with men who probably could have been useful partners.

Even though Milton's influence was formidable, the Wright siblings felt free to make decisions without consulting the bishop. Wilbur's decision to conduct flying experiments at Kitty Hawk wasn't revealed to Milton—who was out of town—until September 3, 1900, just three days before his departure. Milton wasn't told of Orville's involvement until two days later.

And Milton seems to have taken little notice of his sons' early aviation adventures. Until after 1903, the two are scarcely mentioned in his diaries. Once their success was secured, he took more notice of their affairs. "Wilbur and Orville went to work on their Flyer," he wrote on May 27, 1904. "Wilbur and Orville completed the reconstruction. . . ." he reported on July 30. A few days later, "Wilbur made two flights of 800 and 1,304 feet respectively, & Orville one of 640 ft. The speed was 35 to 40 miles to the hour."

Milton retired from the church in 1905. He took his first and only plane ride—a seven-minute excursion over Huffman Prairie outside Dayton—with Orville in 1910. He died in 1917 at the age of 88.

Chapter Eleven

The other brothers

Reuchlin Wright
Lib. of Cong., Prints & Photos Div. LC-DIG-pprs-00482v

Reuchlin was the first-born child of Milton and Susan in 1861. He was born on the family farm (in Grant County, Indiana) Milton had purchased before his marriage. According to biographer Fred Howard, Milton was a circuit preacher at the time who farmed and taught school to supplement his meager church income.

Six years older than Wilbur and ten years older than Orville, Reuch, as he was called by the family, did not share strong ties with his youngest siblings. As young men, though, they appear to have shared some social interests. Reuch was a member of the Ten Dayton Boys, a social club to which his brothers Lorin and Wilbur also belonged.

At the time Wilbur and Orville began their aeronautical experiments in Kitty Hawk, Reuchlin, at 39, lived in Kansas City, Missouri, with his wife, Lulu, and three children, Helen, Herbert and Bertha. He worked as a bookkeeper and then a farmer in the Kansas City area.

He had only limited contact with his family in Ohio—by his own choice, it seems. Letters from Katharine to her father reveal some sort of rift that left Reuch "suspicious of everything." This did not keep him from attending the two-day homecoming extravaganza thrown in his brothers' honor by the city of Dayton in 1908. And he traveled to Dayton when told that Wilbur was critically ill in 1912.

Even so, his alienation from the family was evident. According to Crouch, after Wilbur's death, Reuch returned $1,000 of the bequest he shared equally with his siblings, saying his conscience wouldn't allow him to keep it.

Reuchlin died in 1920.

The Wrights' second child, Lorin, was born in 1862. Although the family still lived on the Grant County farm, Lorin was born in his paternal grandparents' home in Fayette County, Indiana.

Only 20 months younger than Reuch, Lorin was closest to his older brother. He had followed Reuch to Kansas in the 1880s but returned to Dayton after his mother died in 1889. He married his childhood sweetheart, Ivonette (called Netta by the family). Lorin and Netta had four children: Milton, Ivonette, Leontine and Horace. Lorin also worked as a bookkeeper and occasionally helped Wilbur and Orville in their early printing and bicycle businesses.

For part of his adult life, Lorin lived only a block from his father's home on Hawthorn Street. Milton's diaries are full of references to the comings and goings between Lorin's household and his own. Even after Milton, Katharine and Orville moved to Hawthorn Hill in the Oakwood section of the city, the families remained in close contact.

Lorin's children spent much time with their aunt and uncles and their reminiscences of the Wrights provide most of the personal insights into the day-to-day lives of these very private people.

In 1902, Lorin visited Kitty Hawk, in Crouch's words, "to see for himself what his brothers were up to." In 1903, Lorin was given responsibility for releasing the first official notice of his brothers' successful flights to the press. He visited Kitty Hawk again in 1911 while Orville was testing an automatic control device there. When Wilbur and Orville traveled to market the Wright Flyer, Lorin was left in charge of the family businesses which initially included bicycles and airplanes. After Orville got out of the airplane business, Lorin invested in Dayton real estate and, in the 1920s, ran a small company that manufactured toys invented and patented by Orville. He died in 1939.

Lorin Wright
Lib. of Cong., Prints & Photos Div.
LC-DIG-pprs-00499v

Chapter Twelve

Katharine

Katharine Wright
Lib. of Cong., Prints & Photos Div. LC-DIG-pprs-00470v

Katharine Wright (called "Swes" by her brothers and "Kate" by her father) was the only living daughter and last child of Milton and Susan Wright. She was born in 1874, in the West Dayton family home on Hawthorn Street just as her brother Orville had been three years before. She shared his birthday, August 19.

The late 1800s were a time when family ties were valued and family responsibilities considered sacred. Unmarried women often stayed within the family circle. So it was not unusual that Katharine lived at home with her father and two older, bachelor brothers. It was odd, however, that this attractive and socially adept young woman from a good family spent four years at Oberlin College and returned home with a college degree and no husband.

She graduated from Oberlin in 1898. In December of that year, Katharine was called to Steele High School in Dayton as a substitute teacher. In January 1899, she applied for the position of librarian at the school but was told the job had been filled.

According to Milton Wright's diary, Katharine didn't secure a full-time teaching job until January 1900. For the next eight years, she taught history and Latin at the high school. Once she was teaching full-time, Katharine hired 14 year-old Carrie Kayler to help with cleaning and cooking at home.

Katharine, by her own admission, wasn't a great cook. She was fortunate that Orville and Wilbur held fairly liberated views about household skills and were both experienced in the kitchen. Before Carrie came to work for the family, the two brothers took turns cooking in Katharine's absence. They were also handy with a sewing machine. Even so, biographers give Katharine credit for being more than a nominal housekeeper.

From all reports, she was very involved in the management of her home and somewhat intolerant when instructions weren't followed.

Katharine probably chafed in her early role as housemother for the domineering Milton. In spite of the fact that Milton wanted his daughter to have a college education, it seems he never sought her help or advice but relied heavily on Wilbur and sometimes Orville to assist with his editorial and legal duties. Even though it was typical of the times, the attitude would have grated on a capable and educated woman.

Katharine's role in her brother's lives is even more complex. They discussed their plans with her, but she was probably given no say in what they did and little credit for her considerable contributions. Some early biographers reported that Katharine provided money for her brothers' experiments but most historians now dismiss those reports.

What Katharine *did* do was free Orville and Wilbur from the distractions of everyday life. She kept their wardrobes mended and clean, helped manage their schedules, saw that their meals were nutritious and prepared in a timely manner, and provided an orderly, well-kept house.

According to Crouch, "Katharine found real satisfaction in her father's house, but there can be no doubt that the Wright men were the primary beneficiaries of the arrangement. Milton could continue his church work, crisscrossing the country and fighting his battles, confident that the haven to which he had always returned was in the best of hands. Wilbur and Orville enjoyed the benefits of life within a warm and stable family, while escaping the responsibilities that consumed the time and energy of married men. Katharine . . . paid a considerable physical and psychological price. It was her most important and least recognized contribution to the work of the Wright brothers."

Katharine turned 26 in 1900. In addition to managing the home, by most reports, she helped manage the various printing and bicycle businesses the two brothers opened (and closed) before deciding to take on the quest to fly. She also served as hostess for the men, although before the brothers became famous, guests other than family were infrequent. When Wilbur hosted the Annual Club of Ten Dayton Boys (his only known social affiliation at the time) in 1900 at the Hawthorn Street home,

Katharine supervised and attended the dinner as his guest. Milton's position as bishop brought social obligations, but he did most of his socializing outside the home.

Katharine is an integral part of the Wright brothers' life story, but relatively little has been written about her. Some biographers acknowledge her role (Crouch does the best job in *The Bishop's Boys*) while others (notably Fred Kelly in the only biography authorized by Orville Wright) downplay or ignore her significance.

It is interesting to note that during Orville's lifetime, two stories frequently appeared in newspapers and journals—and later in books—crediting Katharine with financing her brothers' flying endeavors and with assisting them with mathematical calculations. Kelly takes time to refute both.

"Another story was that their sister Katharine had furnished the money they needed out of her salary as school teacher," wrote Kelly in *The Wright Brothers*. "Katharine Wright was always amused over that tale, for she was never a hoarder of money nor a financier, and could hardly have provided funds even if this had been necessary. . . . [This] was almost as funny to Katharine as another report—that her brothers had relied on her for mathematical assistance in their calculations," he continued.

Whether Kelly wrote these denials at Orville's request or because he knew the allegations to be untrue—and what Katharine herself had to say about these rumors—is unknown. While Milton, Orville and Wilbur all kept diaries, Katharine evidently did not.

No existing biography of the Wrights provides evidence to support either story about Katharine's contributions. Although both stories continue to be repeated in articles about her, their longevity may have more to do with the scarcity of details about her life than with their validity.

Whatever role she played, it changed dramatically in September 1908. Wilbur was in France trying to sell the Wright Flyer to French investors while Orville was demonstrating their airplane to the U.S. War Department at Ft. Myer, Virginia. Orville's plane crashed. As soon as Katharine got word, she took a leave of absence from Steele High School and rushed to his side. She stayed in Washington, D.C. for six weeks, returned to Dayton with Orville for another month, and then accompanied him to France. She never taught school again.

Katharine was well-suited for helping her brothers market their aeroplane to the world. She was educated, socially graceful and far more gregarious than either brother. John McMahon, an early biographer of the Wrights, credited her with an exceptional memory for names and faces.

As a high school teacher in Dayton, Katharine led an independent social life, in spite of her family's isolationist ways and her responsibilities as manager of their household. Although it appears that she never dated at home, she saw college friends on a regular basis.

She was an active member of the Young Women's League of Dayton, a group founded in the late 1890s by former members of the local YWCA. Not unlike the Y, the group sought to promote moral, mental and physical welfare. She joined the Helen Hunt Club, a group of Dayton school teachers who studied and produced literary works including an annual play. She was also active in the Oberlin College Alumni Association and later served on the college board of trustees.

Equally at ease with men as women, it seems Katharine was accepted in aeronautical circles. Katharine and Orville joined Wilbur in France in January 1909 where Katharine took her first airplane ride. After a couple months, the Wrights traveled to Rome and then on to London. In early May, they returned to the United States. When a special luncheon for Wilbur and Orville was held at a club in Washington, D.C. later that year, the club's 'men only' rule was set aside so that Katharine could attend.

She was "a career woman with moderately feminist views," according to Crouch, but managed to win over most of the men with whom her brothers did business. She was admired in Europe for "her wit and wisdom," he wrote. "King Alfonso [of Spain] pronounced her 'the ideal American.' Most of Europe agreed."

Katharine returned to Europe with Orville in August 1909. They spent the next two months in Germany, then traveled to Paris before returning to the United States in November.

After Wilbur's death in 1912, Katharine frequently accompanied

Orville on business trips throughout the United States. Described by his family as extremely shy and uncomfortable in the limelight, Orville now relied on Katharine to help him through the dozens of dinners and other social gatherings he was expected to attend each year. In 1913, they returned to London and Berlin. Most historians consider this trip Orville's (and probably Katharine's) last to Europe. Some family sources place Orville and Katharine in LeMans, France, in 1920, for the dedication of the Wilbur Wright Monument.

Exactly what Katharine did between traveling with Orville and playing hostess at Hawthorn Hill, the new home she, Orville and Milton moved into in 1913, is unclear. Orville had a secretary, Mabel Beck, so Katharine's role may have been more managerial. Or, perhaps, running the now 15 room Georgian mansion with its 17 acres became a full time job, even though the Wrights employed a husband-and-wife team to handle cooking, cleaning and other chores.

Katharine remained at Hawthorn Hill until November 1926 when she married Henry J. Haskell, a widower. He had attended Oberlin College with Katharine and married her girlfriend. They remained close over the years, eventually serving on the Oberlin College board of trustees together. Knowing that the news of her impending marriage would not be well-received by Orville, now the patriarch of the family, Katharine kept her engagement secret for a year. Orville was furious when he was finally told. The wedding was held at the college, presumably because Orville denied her the use of Hawthorn Hill, and Orville did not attend. Katharine moved to Kansas City.

The rift between brother and sister continued until Katharine came down with a fatal case of pneumonia two years later. After other family members intervened, Orville took the train to Kansas City and saw Katharine on her death bed. She was buried in the family plot in Dayton.

Chapter Thirteen

Will & Orv

Wilbur was born on April 16, 1868, on the family farm outside Millville, Indiana. Orville was born on August 19, 1871, during the Wrights' first residence in Dayton. After a childhood of moving between

Wilbur Wright
Lib. of Cong., Prints & Photos Div.
LC-DIG-pprs-00676v

farms and cities in Indiana, Ohio and Iowa, it's little wonder the two brothers would prefer to stay put once they were grown.

Wilbur attended high school in Richmond, Indiana, and in Dayton. Although some historians credit him with completing his high school education, others say he fell short. In any case, he never received a high school diploma. Orville, less interested in a formal education than Wilbur, dropped out of high school before his senior year to concentrate on the printing business he had started in his early teens.

Wilbur and Orville were the only Wright children not to attend college. Wilbur intended to go to Yale University and for several years after abandoning that plan talked about continuing his education. But until he focused his energies on flying, Wilbur lacked the drive to accomplish his goals in life. The bicycle business provided a comfortable living but it was clearly not what he had in mind. "I do not think I am specially fitted for success in any commercial pursuit," wrote Wilbur to his father in 1894. "I entirely agree that the boys of the Wright family are all lacking in determination and push," he wrote to his sister-in-law in 1901. "None of us has as yet made particular use of the talent in which he excels other men."

Part of Wilbur's inertia probably stemmed from depression. Although it wasn't diagnosed as such at the time, his family—and Wilbur him-self—recognized his blue moods and considered his physical condition fragile. His first recorded bout with depression occurred when Wilbur was 19. A minor ice hockey injury set off a round of heart palpitations and digestive disorders causing Wilbur to give up his plans to attend Yale. For months afterward he stayed home reading and, in the words of his older brother Lorin, playing "cook and chambermaid."

From that point on, Wilbur and his family referred to his health as uncertain. That fragility was no doubt a reflection of his mental state. According to Crouch, Wilbur considered himself a "potential invalid." Wilbur's uncle, William Wright, following a short illness, suffered simi-lar problems that lasted throughout his life. Perhaps the family believed Wilbur was destined by genetics to follow in William's footsteps. As he matured and achieved success with the aeroplane, his tendency for melancholy seems to have diminished. He acknowledged his experience when he wrote to a friend suffering from depression, "Quit it. It does you no good, and it does do harm."

There is speculation, however, that Wilbur was unable to heed his own advice. He had devoted most of his time during the months pre-ceding his untimely death to legal battles over Wright patents. With no end to the litigation in sight, he was said to have been mentally worn down and brooding and when illness overtook him, it is possible that he simply didn't have the will to live.

Orville as young man
Lib. of Cong., Prints & Photos Div. LC-DIG-pprs-00536v

Orville was more good-natured and upbeat. In 1901, when biographers assume Wilbur suffered another bout of depression after spending two months on the Outer Banks, it was Orville who kept the summer in proper perspective. While Wilbur com-plained about faulty data and failed experi-ments and made dour predictions for the future of flight, Orville worked on figuring out what went wrong. After starting wind tunnel tests of airfoils on his own, proving that they could create their own accurate data base, he was able to draw Wilbur back into the process of invention.

As an entrepreneur and inventor, Orville had his own weaknesses. He was a tinkerer and mechanical problem-solver but business was of little interest to him except for the opportunities it gave him to follow his whims. According to Kelly, Orville launched one of his first businesses at the age of 12, when he organized the WJ & M Circus. He failed to promote the event and Wilbur stepped in, writing and distributing a press release that garnered considerable attention. It was their most successful early collaboration.

Shortly thereafter, Orville became interested in the art of printing and started a printing business. Wilbur, once again, stepped in to try to make the venture self-supporting. When interest in that waned and Orville discovered bicycle racing, he and Wilbur opened a bicycle shop. Once they built a successful flying machine, Orville did little to improve the Wright Flyer in spite of the technical advances made by dozens of other aeroplane builders who quickly followed—and surpassed—his lead. After Wilbur's death in 1912, Orville had no interest in running an airplane company; he piloted his last plane in 1918, and he made few contributions of any consequence to aviation.

Wilbur and Orville understood their need to work as a team. After 1900, the brothers were very careful to refer to all their accomplishments as joint efforts and made no distinction between what each man contributed to the mechanical aspects of flight. Officially, all of their accomplishments—mechanical and theoretical—were teamwork. But in private correspondence, Wilbur almost always referred to the theoretical work and calculations as his own. It seems most likely that Wilbur took the lead in posing theoretical questions, while Orville's strength lay in turning theory into practical application. The wind tunnel tests mentioned above were the perfect example of how they worked: The idea to generate their own data was proposed by Wilbur but was made possible only by Orville's ingenuity and mechanical skill. The resulting weeks of testing dozens of airfoil shapes and recording hundreds of measurements provided the breakthrough the Wrights needed for success.

The Wrights' forte was as much adaptation as it was invention. They were not brilliant theorists but exceptional engineers. "Wilbur and Orville did not set out to discover the theoretical principles of flight in the same sense that Newton or Einstein sought to explain physical phenomena in nature. The Wrights' work focused explicitly on determining the design features required to make an airplane fly," wrote Peter Jakab in *Visions of a Flying Machine*. Their goal was less to understand "why a plane would fly than to learn how" and then use the information to build a successful flying machine.

It would be wrong, however, to not acknowledge that some of their most important work was theoretical. They broke new ground in the science of air propulsion when they devised a formula "to understand the effects of a propeller in its operation and thus enable them to design and build, at their first try, the best propeller for the transmission of power," wrote Harry Combs in *Kill Devil Hill*. "There is no way that one can over-dramatize what the Wrights accomplished in their propeller design."

Orville Wright, age 34
Lib. of Cong., Prints & Photos Div.
LC-DIG-pprs-00681v

In a personality profile published in the June 1983 edition of *Aviation, Space and Environmental Medicine*, doctors David Tipton and Stanley Mohler asserted: "A team was formed in which the whole was greater than the sum of its parts . . . Either one, working individually, would probably have been a failure."

Wilbur Wright, age 38
Lib. of Cong., Prints & Photos Div.
LC-DIG-pprs-00682v

"Neither could have mastered the problem alone," wrote Milton, their father, about their aeronautical success. "They are inseparable as twins, they are indispensable to each other."

Wilbur concurred: "From the time we were little children, my brother Orville and myself lived together, played together, worked together, and, in fact, thought together. We usually owned all of our toys in common, talked over our thoughts and aspirations so that nearly everything that was done in our lives has been the result of conversations, suggestions, and discussions between us."

Among family, their arguments were legendary. Well-versed in legal and parliamentary procedure, the two debated every scientific theory and plan of action in every enterprise they undertook. "We don't hear anything but flying machine and engine from morning till night," wrote Katharine to her father after her brothers returned from their second visit to Kitty Hawk in 1901. "I'll be glad when school begins so I can escape."

The arguing got hot and heavy at times. "They'd shout at each other something terrible," said their mechanic Charlie Taylor in an interview years later. "Both the boys had tempers, but no matter how angry they ever got, I never heard them use a profane word." The Wrights appear to have avoided all of the common vices. They didn't swear, smoke, drink, or gamble.

And neither man showed an interest in romance. Neither married. Orville may have considered marriage to a close friend of Katharine's soon after the brothers opened their bicycle shop. It's purely speculation; he refused to confirm or deny the rumor. The history of manned flight might have been considerably different had Orville popped the question and become a husband. Historians believe the technological breakthroughs that made the Wright brothers' accomplishment in 1903 possible were, without doubt, the result of their unfettered collaboration.

As to their creative abilities, Wilbur wrote to a friend, "Very often what you take for some special quality of mind is merely facility arising from constant practice. . . . It is a characteristic of all our family to be able to see the weak points of anything, but this is not always a desirable quality as it makes us too conservative for successful business men, and limits our friendships to a very limited circle."

Rather than calling the brothers "twin-like," it might be better to view their relationship as symbiotic. Their strengths and weaknesses complemented each other. In many ways, they were almost opposites.

Lorin's daughter, Ivonette Wright, spent most Sundays during her childhood at the house on Hawthorn Street. She remembered that "Wilbur never cared much about his appearance, though he liked to look neat and have the proper clothes for the occasion. . . . [He] was quiet, often uncommunicative. When he had something on his mind he would cut himself off from everyone. At times he was unaware of what was going on around him. He was a constant reader. . . . He wrote with great simplicity and clarity. Writing was a pleasure to him." His letters to family members and friends were often filled with dry, witty observations.

Lorin Wright holding three of his children
Lib. of Cong., Prints & Photos Div.
LC-DIG-pprs-00471v

"Wilbur was an independent thinker and leader," said Ivonette in her book of reminiscences published in 1978. "He took the initiative to make some decisions as Orville's older brother . . . he had an unusual presence. Even before men knew who he was, they were drawn to him."

Wilbur "was a gifted public speaker who never failed to delight an audience," wrote Crouch in *The Bishop's Boys*.

"Orville was different," said Ivonette. "He was very conscious of his appearance. . . . He was a dreamer and idealist, quick to see why things didn't work and full of ideas as to how he could improve their efficiency. He was shy and polite, almost to a fault. . . . Uncle Orv liked to work with materials he had on hand. . . . He was artistic. . . . He hated to write letters. Writing was agony to him, although he was very descriptive and detailed when he did."

His family remembered Orville as a flamboyant prankster, a practical joker and tease. He was "a constant talker" at home with family and friends, said Ivonette, but was painfully shy among strangers. Even after 40 years in the public eye, according to Crouch, "he would not so much as offer an after-dinner thank you."

Sundays with her uncles were full of entertainment, according to

Ivonette. They read books aloud, staged shadowgraph shows, played charades and sang songs. Orville "never seemed to tire of playing with us," she wrote. "If he ran out of games, he would make candy . . . Wilbur would amuse us in an equally wholehearted way, but not for long."

Parlor of the Wright home on Hawthorn Street
Lib. of Cong., Prints & Photos Div. LC-DIG-pprs-00539v

For most of their partnership, probably due to Orville's shyness, Wilbur served as the front man. But he was not, by any stretch of the imagination, a social animal. Although both men were often described by their contemporaries as formal and, sometimes, aloof, they were usually considered gracious hosts and men with a good sense of humor. It was not such a bad combination of traits: They were well-liked by most who met them.

By the end of 1905, the brothers' work together as inventors was essentially finished. They were less successful as a marketing team. In this arena, they reinforced each other's inherent mistrust of their fellow man. Rather than hold public exhibitions and announce their invention to the world through usual channels, they remained secretive because they feared others would steal their ideas. Potential customers were not allowed to view the machine or see it in operation until they signed a contract. Although the Wrights' fears were not completely unfounded, most considered their terms unreasonable.

The terms bore Wilbur's imprint, but his letter to Orville, written in February 1907, makes it clear that even in these matters they shared responsibility: "If you think we could enter into a contract for a smaller number of machines than 50, write at once giving your idea of the minimum. Would you be willing . . . to furnish 12 machines for $200,000? I . . . will not attempt to agree to anything along such lines without word from you."

From 1906 until Wilbur's death in 1912, business often kept the brothers apart. Wilbur did most of the traveling abroad while Orville handled negotiations and supervised construction at home. Wilbur usually wrote detailed instructions about tasks Orville needed to accomplish in his absence. They exchanged telegrams and letters almost daily to keep each other updated on their progress.

During the last five years of Wilbur's life, the Wrights' calendar was filled with prestigious meetings, flying demonstrations, state dinners and other forms of public recognition. They hobnobbed with kings, princes, lords, prime ministers and presidents. To most of the outside world, the brothers were enjoying well-deserved success.

"I never knew more simple, unaffected people than Wilbur, Orville, and Katharine," Arthur Harmsworth, Lord Northcliffe, owner of the *London Daily Mail,* said after Orville's death. "I don't think the excitement and interest produced by their extraordinary feat had any effect on them at all."

It does seem that all this attention did little to change the kind of people they were. Orville remained shy, continuing to refuse public speaking engagements; Wilbur remained unsettled, still pursuing his private vision of success.

The idea that he and Orville were not getting all the credit and respect due their invention was close to becoming an obsession for Wilbur. Several inventors tried to take credit for parts of their work: Some, like Augustus Herring, had modest ties to the Wrights, and others, like John Montgomery, a Californian claiming the wing-warping discovery, had none. A tribute to Samuel Langley, published in a respected journal after his death, gave Langley credit, incorrectly, for helping the Wright brothers. Chanute, the Wrights' former mentor, chided Wilbur for not being more generous in sharing his knowledge. Published reports claimed others had flown before 1903. Wilbur felt compelled to take note of every assault. If he couldn't respond personally, he often directed his lawyers to take action. Even the most generous biographers note that the Wrights were constantly embroiled in legal battles.

Writing to a friend in January 1912, Wilbur spoke of wanting to be free from lawsuits and business matters which had consumed his time for several years. "When we think what we might have accomplished if we had been able to devote this time to experiments, we feel very sad, but it is always easier to deal with things than with men, and no one can direct his life entirely as he would choose."

Family members describe Wilbur as "tired" and "white" during his last months. He was diagnosed with typhoid fever on May 2, 1912. He died on May 30 at home on Hawthorn Street in Dayton, surrounded by his family. He was 45.

With Katharine's help after Wilbur's death, Orville spent the next few years wrapping up legal matters and getting out of the flying machine business. He got back into the airplane business once more with the formation of the Wright-Dayton Co. in 1917, but his heart was not in it. He preferred to spend time in his private workshop, tinkering with a variety of projects that ranged from household gadgets to possible weapons of war. He continued to make public appearances (though not speeches), served on committees and boards of directors but in general did little of note except lend the prestige of the Wright name to benefit aviation.

Orville (standing, left), Katharine and Milton Wright (seated in front of Orville), on the porch at Hawthorn Hill

Lib. of Cong., Prints & Photos Div. LC-DIG-pprs-00754v

Orville, Katharine and Milton moved to Hawthorn Hill in 1914. The 17-acre property in Oakwood, a southern suburb of Dayton, was selected and purchased by Wilbur for the family before his death. Orville lived there until a heart attack ended his life in 1948 at the age of 77.

Preparing to Fly

An ad for the Wright Cycle Co. run in the High School Times, *1897*

Chapter Fourteen

An early interest

Some years after the Wright brothers flew at Kitty Hawk, Wilbur wrote that he and Orville "became seriously interested in the problem of human flight in 1899. . . . Our own growing belief that man might learn to fly was based on the idea that while thousands of the most dissimilar body structures, such as insects, fish, reptiles, birds and mammals, were flying every day at pleasure, it was reasonable to suppose that man might also fly."

"Our first interest began when we were children," wrote Orville in *How We Invented the Airplane.* "Father brought home to us a small toy actuated by a rubber string which would lift itself into the air. We built a number of copies of this toy, which flew successfully. . . ."

As young men the Wrights played with a toy similar to this ornithopter designed by the French engineer, Alphonse Pénaud.

In 1896, they read about the exploits of Otto Lilienthal, a German experimenting with gliders. His death, after such well-publicized success, sent the brothers looking for more information about the science of flight. "We found a work written by Professor Marey on animal mechanism which treated of the bird mechanism as applied to flight," said Orville. "But other than this, so far as I can remember, we found little."

Orville evidently turned his attention back to the bicycles and his new passion, motor cars. According to Crouch, Orville and a friend, who owned one of the new gasoline-powered marvels, "fiddled with the machine for hours, discussing the intricacies of ignition, carburetion, and differential gearing systems." At the time, he had no way of knowing how valuable this interest in engines would become.

Chapter Fifteen

The perfect start

The bicycle business Orville and Wilbur began in 1893 provided them with a decent living. They were independent business owners taking home over $1,000 each a year when the average Dayton factory worker made less than $500. The men worked with their hands, but it was a far cry from farming, mining or working in the meat-packing plants, machine shops and steel mills as did most of their peers. In 1896, the same year Lilienthal died, the Wrights designed and began manufacturing their own line of bicycles, a more satisfying enterprise for two inventive entrepreneurs.

It was evidently not satisfying enough for Wilbur, who continued to ponder the possibility of tackling the problem of manned flight himself. Whether he realized bicycles would soon be replaced by automobiles or whether he simply fancied a more singular role for himself than being one of dozens of other back-room bicycle makers in the city, the bicycle business was, nonetheless, one that proved invaluable to his future.

At first thought, it might seem that bicycles and airplanes have little in common. But, in fact, the first motorized airplane to carry man aloft owed its very existence to bicycle design and technology. As inventors, the Wrights worked with what they knew—and what they knew was bicycles.

It is doubtful they could have a better preparation for the work they were about to begin. College would have been of little help. At the time they left high school, on the heels of the Industrial Revolution, most schools offered few, if any, courses in modern engineering, applied physics and mechanical science. The resources to teach anything at all about flight were limited. Research that supported aerodynamics and the science of propulsion, lift and air pressures was rudimentary. Books about flight, as Orville noted above, were hard to find. Chanute's *Progress in Flying Machines*, the most comprehensive study of man's attempts to fly, had just been published.

The idea that airplanes might evolve from bicycles made its debut in 1896, when a New York newspaper editor predicted bicycle makers would be the first to successfully build a heavier-than-air flying machine. The technology that would produce a swift bicycle would eventually produce something with wings that could fly, he wrote. He was right: When the Wrights set their sights on flying, they used many of the same materials, techniques and engineering principles used in their bicycles to build their gliders and airplanes.

Much has been made of Wilbur's eureka moment while twisting a long, thin, bicycle inner tube box. For weeks he and Orville had been arguing over how to control the lateral movements of a theoretical aeroplane. "They were agreed in practice, at least, that if they could change the angle at which the wing attacked the air, and change it rapidly and with reliable response, they would gain an element of control," wrote Harry Combs in his book, *Kill Devil Hill*. They were unable to devise any workable idea for accomplishing this until Wilbur pressed the corners of the box slightly

Wilbur Wright, working at a lathe in his bicycle shop
Lib. of Cong., Prints & Photos Div. LC-DIG-pprs-00540v

together and twisted them in opposite directions. His mind's eye saw the top and bottom of the box as the upper and lower wing surfaces of a biplane; the helicoidal twist presenting the different angles on the left and right sides. "From this it was apparent that the wings of a machine . . . could be warped so as to present their surfaces to the air at different angles of incidence and thus secure unequal lifts on the two sides," explained Orville in *How We Invented the Airplane*. Wing-warping and its consequence, unequal lift, allowed the machine to be turned at the operator's discretion—the one control problem previous builders of flying machines had been unable to solve. But the role bicycles played in the Wrights' success was greater than that one coincidence.

When the Wrights built bicycles, they offered customers their choice of metal wheels or wooden ones, steamed and shaped in their shop. They employed the same techniques to construct the ribbed wings of their gliders. The Wrights weren't the first to use ribbed wings, but many early aviators did not. Wing instability had contributed to several spectacular failures.

Much of the wire and many of the fittings on the Wright gliders and early powered machines were borrowed from bicycles. When they built their first powered machine, they used the double triangle frame from their Van Cleve bicycle. They used bicycle chain to transfer power from the small motor to the propeller and to run the water pump.

More importantly, their concept of balance—and the involvement of the pilot in keeping a flying machine in balance—was a direct consequence of their own experience riding and designing bicycles.

Once the brothers understood how to control a flying machine, they progressed to adding a motor. They relied on what they'd learned tinkering with a motor-powered line shaft in their bicycle shop. With the help of their mechanic, Charlie Taylor, they were able to build the gasoline engine they needed.

The bicycle business also gave the two a chance to work out the kinks in their business relationship. By the time they began developing their airplane, they understood how to work together. Quite possibly, they realized that their real genius was to be found in the interplay of their individual talents. The ego-less public partnership, the "Wright Brothers" signature that gave neither man precedence over the other, was the result of nearly a decade's worth of experience at handling their close—and often competitive—relationship.

Chapter Sixteen

Wilbur's quest

Historians believe that Wilbur, alone, had the serious interest in pursuing manned flight—and that he later talked Orville into the venture. The Wrights' father, Milton, came to the same conclusion. But, not given to personal revelation, neither brother ever addressed this issue.

It was Wilbur who began their research by writing to the Smithsonian Institution in May 1899, asking for aeronautical information. The Smithsonian received his letter on June 2 and the very next day posted a reply. The following week he sent an order for reading material. In three months, he read every book and technical article about previous attempts at flight and aeronautical theory that he could find. Whether or not Orville had bought into the quest at this time, Wilbur undoubtedly shared some of this information with him. It was their habit to clarify critical thinking through argument with each other.

By the time Wilbur finished his reading, he had decided control was the one thing no aviation pioneer had yet mastered. Many, in fact, claimed that flying machines should have "automatic control," an idea he rejected out of hand. He believed from the outset of his experiments that operator control would be the key to manned, powered flight—and he was right.

By mid-summer, the two brothers had built a five-foot biwing kite and were testing some of their ideas about control. With those results in hand, they made plans to build a full-size glider and find a suitable, windy place to try their hand at gliding.

On November 27, 1899, Wilbur wrote to the U.S. Weather Bureau, requesting wind information. On December 4, the Bureau sent to him the August and September issues of the *Monthly Weather Review*, which listed average hourly wind velocities at all 120 weather stations then operating in the United States. Kitty Hawk, North Carolina, was included on the list. It seems likely this was the Wrights' first glimpse of the name of the place that would be forever linked with theirs.

In May 1900, 33-year-old Wilbur wrote to Octave Chanute, an aviation pioneer old enough to be his grandfather. Chanute had authored two
books on flying machines, designed gliders and supervised their testing
on the shores of Lake Michigan. He was respected in aviation circles
worldwide and was well-known as a mentor for up-and-coming aeronautical experimenters.

In his letter, Wilbur shared his plans for flying experiments and asked
Chanute's advice about a suitable location. He had already come to the
conclusion that Dayton didn't have enough wind; Chicago, the nation's
windiest city, had too many people.

Chanute responded that he "preferred preliminary learning on a sand
hill and trying ambitious feats over water." He mentioned San Diego,
California, and St. James City or Pine Island, Florida. Some other spot on
the Atlantic coast of South Carolina or Georgia might be preferable, he
suggested. He also agreed that the brothers would be better off if they
avoided attracting crowds.

California and Florida were too far from Dayton for Wilbur. He went
back to the U.S. Weather Bureau list: Kitty Hawk, with an average wind
of 13.4 mph, ranked sixth in the nation. On August 3, 1900, he wrote a
letter to the Kitty Hawk weather station requesting more detailed information about the area. By the end of the month he had two replies, a brief
response from Joseph Dosher, the only employee at the Kitty Hawk
weather station and a longer letter from William Tate, a gregarious vil-
lager with whom Dosher had shared Wilbur's inquiry. Tate's letter, full of
flowery descriptions about the lay of the land and assurances of ideal
winds, included an offer of hospitality too good for Wilbur to ignore. It
wasn't the first piece of puffery written about the Outer Banks but it was
destined to become one of the most famous.

Correspondence was Wilbur's lifeline to information. He had no
access to academic or professional circles that might have nurtured or
supported the experiments he wanted to undertake. He never attended any
symposium on flight or personally viewed any experimental aircraft. His
research was conducted by what's known in the 21st century as "snail
mail." He was fortunate ground mail traveled so fast and was answered

so quickly in his day. Air mail, of course, was yet to come.

Biographers describe Wilbur Wright as orderly, goal-oriented, dogged, determined, brilliant, creative. No one ever called him impulsive. But how else would you describe a man who boards a train east, heading to Kitty Hawk, North Carolina, a place he'd only learned about one month earlier? Everything he knew about his destination was contained in the correspondence from Dosher and Tate, two men he had never met. As an adult, the farthest he had ever been from home was Chicago, a 250-mile trip made with Orville in 1893.

It's easy to think of Wilbur's 600-mile trip to Kitty Hawk as a careful step in a well-planned quest. In fact, it was as crazy and risky as the idea of flying itself. And, as if that weren't enough, he took a half-built glider with him on the train and planned to shop for parts on the way.

What plans he cobbled together in such a short time were made without benefit of modern communications. He couldn't log on the Internet to reserve tickets with his VISA card. He couldn't tune into a seven-day weather forecast and travel advisory. There were no Yellow Pages to let his fingers do the walking when it came to finding lumber and other supplies in unfamiliar cities. There would be no phone calls home for moral support, no automatic teller machines to get

Union Station, Dayton, Ohio
Lib. of Cong., Prints & Photos Div. LC-DIG-pprs-4a12177r

cash for unexpected expenses, no hopping a plane and getting home in an hour if things didn't pan out.

When Wilbur left Union Station in Dayton at 6:30 p.m. on September 6, 1900, less than 30 days after getting Bill Tate's invitation to come on down, he set off on a real adventure. Calling him impetuous wouldn't be far off the mark.

Wrights' World, circa 1900

Dayton courthouse in downtown Dayton, c. 1902
Lib. of Cong., Prints & Photos Div. LC-DIG-pprs-4a09909r

Main Street, Dayton, Ohio
c. 1904
Lib. of Cong., Prints & Photos Div.
LC-DIG-pprs-4a12175r

Chapter Seventeen

Dayton, Ohio

The Midwest and its cities are sometimes considered the trailing edge of just
about everything in today's world. "Will it
play in Peoria?"—an Illinois city not
unlike Dayton, Ohio—is a benchmark for
anything new, implying that middle
America can be a hard sell when it comes to trendsetting. It wasn't always
so.

When Wilbur and Orville were growing up in Dayton in the late
1800s, the Midwest was on the leading edge, a frontier. Chicago, incorporated not quite 50 years earlier, was in many ways still a cow town. The
first transcontinental railway had been completed in 1869; the railroad
yards that would put Chicago on the map were still on the drawing board.

Dayton, incorporated in 1805, had a 30-year start on Chicago. Like
most of its contemporaries west of the Appalachians, it went from back-
woods outpost to modern city in less than 100 years. But without
Chicago's Great Lakes port and railroad connections, Dayton would
never become one of the nation's leading cities.

Even so, in the last 20 years of the 19th century, Dayton's population
more than doubled, from 38,600 to 85,000 and, in the Wrights' lifetimes,
it achieved remarkable prosperity. Change, growth, innovation and invention left its mark on everyday life. Ohio's fifth-largest city in 1900 behind
Akron, Cincinnati, Columbus and Toledo, it ranked third in the state for
capital investments.

Barney & Smith Car Co., a manufacturer of wooden railroad cars,
was established in 1849 although demand for steel cars by the turn of the
century dealt the company a serious blow. The cash register was invented by a Dayton saloon keeper in 1878. The invention was purchased by
another Daytonian, James H. Patterson, six years later and became the
keystone of the National Cash Register Co., one of America's greatest

business success stories.

By 1892, Dayton had its first "skyscraper," a nine-story building, and many buildings had electric lights. Natural gas service and manufactured ice were available to city residents. The city's Bell telephone system, established in 1879, served 2,000 subscribers in 1900. A competitor introduced its first automatic switchboard in Dayton and provided service to 6,000 telephones.

According to historian A. W. Drury, the city began paving its streets with granite blocks in 1888. By 1892, all downtown streets were paved, even though automobile traffic wouldn't be commonplace for another 10 years. Daytonians pioneered the use of concrete and steel construction in bridges crossing Great Miami River, which runs through the heart of the city. The city's electric street cars, put into service in 1887, were among the first in municipal use in the United States.

As the 19th century came to a close, Dayton was changing even more. Close proximity to Chicago, now the nation's second largest city, put Dayton directly in the path of progress—and the years spanning the turn of the century proved to be Dayton's time to shine.

In 1901, Dayton's population was nearing 100,000. The city's skyline soared up to 13 stories. The city's 12 daily newspapers brought its citizens news from around the world. Its retailers offered groceries and dry goods rural America once produced for itself while, with the help of new assembly-line technology, its manufacturers turned out cash registers, tires and machine parts along with its farm implements and bicycles. National Cash Register, Davis Sewing Machine and more than 300 other industrial companies employed thousands of workers. The city's precision tool industry was a national leader.

More patents were held by inventors in Dayton than in any other Ohio city. There was probably no other single city of its size responsible for so many inventions that would change the way men and women lived and worked.

By the time the Wrights flew at Kitty Hawk in 1903, Daytonians were inventing the electric starter for gasoline engines and anti-knock gasoline, perfecting the Frigidaire and forming the conglomerate that became

International Business Machines (IBM). John Q. Sherman's Standard Register Corporation, started in Dayton, transformed business record-keeping with its punched, continuous-feed forms and the autographic register.

The city the Wrights called home was an exciting place to be in 1900, a place where the sky and beyond was the limit for two young men with an interest in invention. Dayton, it seemed, had just about everything they could want—except the terrain and weather they needed to test their gliders and bring their dream of manned flight to fruition.

Chapter Eighteen

Kitty Hawk, North Carolina

With advice from aviation pioneer Octave Chanute and statistics from the U.S. Weather Service, Wilbur identified several locations better suited than Dayton for their flying experiments. One of those places was Kitty Hawk, North Carolina.

It could be said that Kitty Hawk was a naive choice, made by a man accustomed to middle class comfort who had never traveled far from home. Wilbur had no idea what life on a sparsely populated barrier island, 600 miles from Dayton, would be like.

When Wilbur arrived at Kitty Hawk in the fall of 1900, the village consisted of nearly 60 houses and over

Soundside woods near Kitty Hawk village c. 1900
Lib. of Cong., Prints & Photos Div. LC-DIG-pprs-00543v

250 people split between what locals called "up the road" and "down the road." The main road through the village ran approximately as Kitty Hawk Road runs today, winding across nearly a dozen dune ridges, down into the low marshland fronting Currituck Sound. "Up the road" was in the lower village, but to the northwest and, thus, "up" from the "down the road" community on the higher ridges to the southeast. At the time, both sections were called Kitty Hawk and were served by a single post office run by the Tates out of their home in the "down the road" community. A few years later, "up the road" was given its own post office with the designation Otilla, but the new name never caught on.

It should be noted that in 1900 Kitty Hawk was part of Currituck County. With no bridges or motorized transportation, the village was cut

off from its seat of government. It wasn't until 1920 that the state legis-
lature adjusted the county lines bringing Kitty Hawk into Dare County. In
1900, the Wrights conducted their experiments just outside Kitty Hawk
village. In 1901 they moved their camp south, near a large sand dune
known as Kill Devil Hill. The present-day town of Kill Devil Hills, which
took its name from the now-famous dune, did not exist at the time. Since
Kitty Hawk was the closest year-round community and the Wrights' usual
source for food, supplies and other services, the first flights were always
said to have taken place at Kitty Hawk—even though today the location
is within the town of Kill Devil Hills.

According to Kitty Hawk historian Bill Harris, each community had
its own church, ungraded school and general store. The up-the-roaders
were Baptists while down-the-roaders worshiped as Methodists. Church
was the "social center of the community," said Harris. Even folks who
didn't consider themselves Baptists or Methodists attended the church
closest to their home. The Tates were members of the Methodist church.
The Wrights were raised in the United Brethren church, a denomination
that later merged with the Methodists, and would have been welcome but
there's no evidence they ever attended church in Kitty Hawk.

There was no electricity, no running water, no telephone service,
although the community had one telegraph. There were no automobiles at
the time and all roads were simply sand tracks. Firewood was at a premi-
um so kerosene was the fuel of choice for both heating and cooking. Oil
lamps were used for light.

The village had no medical doctor. A doctor from the Currituck mainland traveled to the village if summoned but his visits were rare. John
Cogswell, a schooled pharmacist and Bill Tate's brother-in-law, lived in
Kitty Hawk in 1900. Villagers called him "doctor" and it seems likely that
he—along with a couple women who served as midwives—was the medical mainstay. The Wrights, who didn't do a lot of socializing in the village, probably met Cogswell through the Tates. He is mentioned in their
correspondence.

In 1900, the village was populated with families still found in the
local phone book: Baums, Perrys, Harrises, Tilletts, Beachams, Beasleys,

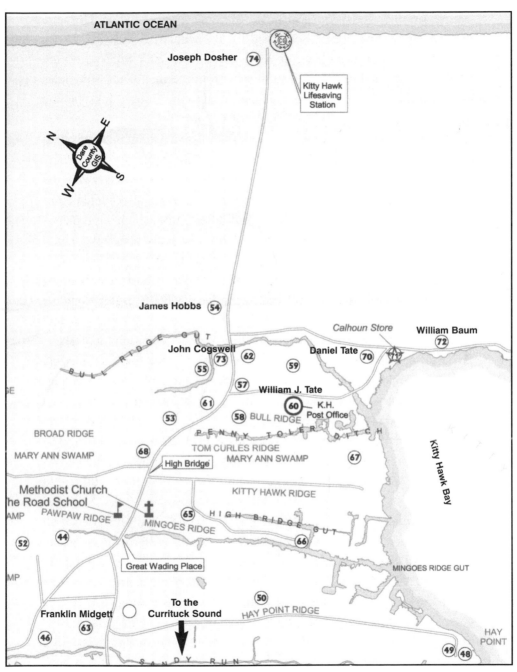

Kitty Hawk, North Carolina, circa 1900
Map courtesy Bill Harris

Hines, Owens, Sawyers, Twifords, Rogers, Tolers, Tates, Doshers, O'Neals and a few others. Some had lived in the area since the 1700s; many had arrived in the last 50 years. Some were shipwrecked on the Banks and decided to stay; others moved from the mainland. Both sides of the Harris family moved from the mainland to the Outer Banks, but the reasons for their moves are lost pieces of history.

In the 1900 census, 40 Kitty Hawk men listed fishing as their occupation. Only 10 listed the lifesaving service as their primary job. Others may have worked at the stations but the service only operated during the winter months in 1900 making it a part-time job. Many also hunted commercially for duck, goose, wild boar and other game which were plentiful on the Outer Banks in those days. Only one Kitty Hawk woman, a dressmaker, listed an occupation in that census, according to Harris.

At the turn of the century, very few Kitty Hawkers had better than the elementary school education offered by the local schools. But it would be wrong to portray the village as illiterate, said Harris. Most could read and write. Although the Wrights were short on formal education themselves, their self-acquired knowledge in the fields of science and engineering, and their single-minded focus on such matters, probably made exchanging more than social pleasantries with villagers difficult—if they even tried. Neither brother was very outgoing. Villagers found the two pleasant and polite but, for the most part, had little to do with them. The Wrights mention socializing only with Tate, Cogswell, Dosher and a few others who were probably a little better informed about the world in general.

Few Kitty Hawkers earned more than $200 or $300 a year. Almost all were subsistence farmers keeping chickens, cows, a horse or mule and plots of potatoes, corn and other vegetables (although growing crops in the sandy soil was nearly impossible). The village's general stores were small and carried very little except absolute necessities that couldn't be grown or handmade at home. Traveling salesmen visited the village a few times a year, said Harris, selling things like sewing machines and iron stoves. Some families may have made shopping trips to Elizabeth City, the nearest town of any size, but such trips were few and far between until around 1905 when gasoline engines made local boat travel faster and more dependable. In 1900, only a few village men had the resources and time to make the trip. When they went, they shopped for the entire community. Orders could also be placed through the general store and brought to the village on the mailboat.

The Wright brothers, accustomed to buying the food and goods they needed, strained the local economy. "The economics of this place were so nicely balanced before our arrival that everybody here could live and yet nothing be wasted," wrote Orville to his sister Katharine after he arrived in Kitty Hawk in October 1900. "Our presence brought disaster to the whole arrangement. . . . There is no store in Kitty Hawk; that is, not anything that you would call a store. Our pantry in its most depleted state would be a mammoth affair compared with our Kitty Hawk stores. Our camp alone exhausts the output of all the henneries within a mile."

The best homes in Kitty Hawk were two-story but small by Dayton standards, unpainted and without any sort of luxury. According to Wilbur, furniture, carpets, books and pictures were scarce. What few photos exist of the village around the turn of the century show simple, wood-frame houses, most akin to farm houses of the era with no adornment except a front porch that usually stretched across the entire front.

There were no rental accommodations in Kitty Hawk. After boarding with the Tates for a short while, Wilbur and Orville set up camp on Lookout Hill, south of the village, where they lived in a tent and did most of their own cooking. Even though both brothers described the living conditions at their Kitty Hawk camp in harsh detail (Orville said it reminded him "of those poor Arctic explorers"), their descriptions showed a bit of Boy Scout enthusiasm. As uncomfortable and inconvenient as life in a tent must have been, they rarely allowed it to interfere with their work.

Although they never seriously considered any other location, the Wrights believed Kitty Hawk was the right place for them to accomplish what they set out to do. They liked the people and the isolation. Being away from Dayton freed their minds from family and business matters and allowed them to concentrate on flying.

Ironically, the weather and wind—the very things that brought them to the Outer Banks—were a continual source of vexation.

"We reached Kitty Hawk several days later than we expected owing to the greatest storm in history of the place. . . ." wrote Wilbur to Chanute on July 26, 1901. "After a dry spell of 7 weeks the storm was followed by rains for a full week. This has delayed us beyond expectation, both by preventing us from working at times, and especially by compelling us to devote a large part of our time to fighting mosquitoes. . . ." The Wrights were only experiencing what many folks—from the earliest explorers to today's tourists—consider one of the few disagreeable aspects of an Outer Banks summer.

At the turn of the century, day-trippers and overnight guests arrived by the dozens during the summer at Nags Head.
Photo courtesy Outer Banks History Center

The more agreeable attractions of the barrier islands were already well-established. Just a few miles south of the Wrights' camp at Kill Devil Hill stood Nags Head, one of the state's most popular summer resorts. Dozens of families from North Carolina's coastal plain spent their entire summers at the shore while hundreds of others from as far away as New York and Pennsylvania came to stay for a week or two at one of several hotels. Steamers brought day-trippers from Elizabeth City six days a week.

North Carolina historian Catherine Bishir quoted the editor of the Elizabeth City *Economist* as saying in 1900 the resort was "one of the most valuable institutions of the Albemarle country," patronized by "most all the citizens of Albemarle, Tar River, and Pamlico sections."

By this time, the string of cottages now known as the "Unpainted Aristocracy" held court on the oceanfront while hotels and boardwalks lined the soundside. The hotels offered horse-drawn carts and railcars to the ocean beach. Climbing Jockey's Ridge was part of the annual pilgrimage. Fishing, bathing (as swimming or wading was called in those days) and sailing in the sound were regular activities. Hotel guests dressed for dinner and enjoyed musical entertainment over drinks afterward.

Nags Head Woods, near Jockey's Ridge and a couple miles south of the Wrights' camp, was considered a separate community. Like Kitty Hawk, it was populated by families who farmed and fished but, unlike their counterparts to the north, many of these locals made a handsome summer living by hauling tourists around the resort and to the beach.

While Kitty Hawkers were no doubt aware of what went on to the south, lack of roads and a different lifestyle kept interaction between the communities at a minimum. In 1900, the Wrights may not have known anything about Nags Head. Arriving in late fall, the summer season would have been over, the hotels and summer homes boarded up for the winter. In 1901, however, they arrived during summer, and it's possible they visited Nags Head that year.

There is no evidence either Wright went to Manteo before 1903. Although Bill Tate, the Kitty Hawk resident who invited Wilbur to come to the Outer Banks to conduct his flying experiments, may have recommended traveling to Kitty Hawk via Manteo in 1900, the Wrights took a different route. Had they followed his advice, they would have been surprised: Manteo, chosen as the county seat in 1874 when Dare County was formed, was a busy place.

Downtown Manteo, c. 1900
Photo courtesy Outer Banks History Center

Long after the Nags Head resort shuttered its doors for winter, boat traffic continued to sail into Shallowbag Bay, just two miles across the Roanoke Sound, to dock at Manteo, Dare County's first incorporated town. Chartered in 1899, Manteo already boasted regular boat service to

Elizabeth City and Norfolk. A new hotel, The Roanoke, advertised as "neat and clean" with "electric bells and indoor closets" for just $1.50 a day, was better appointed than the Wrights' tent in Kitty Hawk. (Such luxury, even if it had been more accessible, would not have appealed to the frugal brothers.)

The population of Manteo was at least 300 with the 1900 census listing 59 houses and 60 families living within its limits. It was a growing community, according to Angel Ellis Khoury, author of *Manteo: A Roanoke Island Town.* And with dressmakers, a lawyer, two doctors, two blacksmiths, and a bookkeeper—along with a wheelwright, milliner, clock repairman and other service providers—it was remarkably cosmopolitan in spite of its isolated location.

Even though the town had several hardware, general merchandise, clothing and grocery stores, the Wrights mention getting supplies only from Elizabeth City during their first visits. Most likely, the time saved by sailing to Manteo rather than Elizabeth City from Kitty Hawk was outweighed by the benefits of shopping in a larger town.

Chapter Nineteen

Elizabeth City, North Carolina

The Norfolk-Southern rail station, c. 1900
Photo courtesy Museum of the Albemarle

In 1900, Elizabeth City was a thriving metropolis by North Carolina standards. In 1880, the city's population had been just 2,300. By the turn of the century, the population was 6,300, thanks, in part, to the opening of the Norfolk-Southern rail line in 1881. Business leaders of the day called the city "The Hub of the Albemarle" as they capitalized on its deep water port and proximity to the Chesapeake Bay through Hampton Roads via a new canal.

Farming, ruined mid-century by the Civil War and breakdown of the plantation system, was once again a thriving enterprise. Cotton, corn, peas, peanuts, tobacco and other agricultural products were shipped out of the city's port along with raw lumber, shingles and other wood products. The Elizabeth City Cotton Mills, opened in 1897, was one of the city's major employers.

When Wilbur stepped off the train at the north edge of Elizabeth City's downtown waterfront in 1900, the first things he probably saw were the tall

Poindexter Street in downtown Elizabeth City c. 1905
Photo courtesy Museum of the Albemarle

brick chimneys of the Knobbs Creek lumber yards. Looking south, he would have seen the Pasquotank County Courthouse whose cupola and clock towered over a low-rise downtown. The First Baptist Church on West Main with its three-story bell tower topped with a large spire and the Methodist Church on East Church Street dominated the three-story sky-line.

By his own report, he checked in at the Arlington Hotel, one of several hotels in the city, and immediately walked to the docks seeking a ride to Kitty Hawk.

As Wilbur walked through downtown, he would have passed the Lowry-Chesson Building at Main and Poindexter, the opera house at Poindexter and Church and the C. H. Robinson Building on South Road Street. Poindexter Street was being guttered and paved that year but most of the city's streets were still dirt. A few were topped with oyster shells, even fewer were cobblestone and brick. The automobile wouldn't make its appearance here until later in the decade.

The Elizabeth City Electric Light Co. had been established in 1892 but electricity was still a novelty here. Local telephone service began in 1894 but long distance service wasn't available until 1902.

Six newspapers were published in the city. The two largest—*The Economist* and the *Fisherman and Farmer*—were the main source of state and national news for the region. These were the only ones regularly distributed on the Outer Banks, arriving by boat with the mail, often several days after they were published.

There were over 150 stores within the city limits, the region's largest bank, several small manufacturers, a YMCA, and a beer bottler. In addition to the railroad, the city was served by two steamer lines and dozens of commercial boats. Although there was service to other North Carolina cities, Norfolk, Virginia, was the most common destination.

Chapter Twenty

Norfolk, Virginia

Old Point Comfort, Virginia, c. 1900
Lib. of Cong., Prints & Photos Div. LC-DIG-pprs-4a15008r

On his first trip to the Outer Banks, Wilbur took the train from Dayton to Old Point Comfort in Newport News where he boarded the steamer *Pennsylvania.* After crossing Hampton Roads on a Friday, he spent the night at the Monticello Hotel in downtown Norfolk.

Historians haven't recorded Wilbur's first impression of Norfolk, and it may be that he never said much about it, but it's easy to imagine how it must have seemed. Compared to Dayton, Norfolk was rough around the edges and still wet behind the ears. Nearby Jamestown was established in 1607, but Norfolk wasn't incorporated until 1845. Since that time, its population had grown from 14,300 to 46,600 according to the 1900 census—only half the size of Dayton.

For years, Norfolk's prospects for prosperity were limited by its swampy ground and reputation for epidemic illness. During the Civil War, although it served as a pivotal military port, the city was virtually cut off from the rest of the state. After the war, the region's agricultural trade grew. In 1900, more than 11 million tons of lumber, produce, fish and oysters, raw cotton and mill goods, peanuts and other cargo were shipped through its port. The Spanish-American war was an economic coup for the city, reaffirming Hampton Roads as a military necessity and its shipyards as first-rate. It was a young city, still growing, and far from polished.

On Saturday, Wilbur walked around downtown, shopping for sup plies and lumber. In 1900, as today, downtown businesses lined the

Elizabeth River. City Hall Avenue, Granby, Tazewell and Brambleton were major thoroughfares. The six-story Monticello Hotel, completed in 1898, was the state's largest and, at the time, dominated its downtown corner—although the seven-story Citizen's Bank Building, next to the U.S. Customhouse on Main Street was the city's tallest. The post office

Waterfront, Norfolk, Virginia, c. 1905
Lib. of Cong., Prints & Photos Div.
LC-DIG-pprs-4a12466r

at Plume and Atlantic was new. So was the Norfolk & Western railway station with its fancy stick work, peaked roofs and clock tower at the corner of Main and Lake. Many of the city's buildings were new, more than 2,900 of them built in the last decade.

Most Norfolk streets, including those plied by the city's new electric street cars, were still unpaved. The automobile had just made its first appearance in the city, but the steam-powered "Locomobile" had caught the local fancy. Bicycles were everywhere.

Wilbur didn't linger after shopping for supplies. He found most of what he needed—except for the 18-foot spruce timbers to build the gliders' wing spars. Then he boarded a train Saturday afternoon headed for Elizabeth City.

On the Outer Banks, 1900

Kitty Hawk Bay viewed from the Wright brothers' 1900 camp
Lib. of Cong., Prints & Photos Div. LC-DIG-pprs-00568v

Chapter Twenty One

The great adventure begins

Wilbur arrived in Elizabeth City on Saturday afternoon, September 8, 1900, and checked into the Arlington Hotel on Water Street. He then walked to the nearby docks to find passage to Kitty Hawk. Three days passed before he found someone willing to carry him, the glider he and Orville designed and other supplies down the Pasquotank River and across the Albemarle Sound.

"No one seemed to know anything about the place or how to get there," wrote Wilbur in his diary. It is likely the locals were simply having a good laugh at the expense of this formally dressed Yankee. It would be hard to imagine any waterman worth his salt who wasn't familiar with the Outer Banks. In any case, the circumstances of his travel are full of contradictions.

Joe Dosher, the Weather Bureau employee who answered Wilbur's inquiry about flying conditions at Kitty Hawk, had written that the only passage to Kitty Hawk would be via Manteo "in a small sail boat." William J. "Bill" Tate, a Kitty Hawk resident followed up Dosher's terse reply with more specific instructions. The August 18, 1900, letter on file at the Library of Congress, clearly stated "You can reach here from Eliz. City N.C. by boat direct or from Manteo 12 miles from here by mail boat every Mon. Wed. & Friday." Other records of the

Kitty Hawk Life-Saving Station, far right, with the tiny U.S. Weather Bureau building to its left

Lib. of Cong., Prints & Photos Div. LC-DIG-pprs-00557r

day indicate the mail boat ran only on Fridays at that time of the year.

But Tate always denied telling Wilbur how he could get to the Outer

Banks. Writing for the *Aeronautic Review* in 1928, he said "I did not say a word about transportation facilities, neither did I give a word of direction about how to get to Kitty Hawk. Mr. Wright never forgot to joke me about this lack of information, which no doubt was impressed on him during the wearisome trip from Elizabeth City to Kitty Hawk."

Whether Wilbur knew about mail service or not, he'd missed the Friday boat and his first attempts to find an alternate ride were unsuccessful. Wilbur never explained why he didn't pursue passage on the mail boat if, indeed, it ran on Monday as Tate said. Finally, on Tuesday afternoon, September 11, he found Israel Perry, a Kitty Hawk native, who agreed to carry him to the village.

Elizabeth City docks, c. 1905
Photo courtesy Museum of the Albemarle

Perry's fishing boat, the *Curlicue*, was anchored three miles downriver from Elizabeth City. Perry and his mate loaded Wilbur, his luggage and lumber into a skiff. The crated half-built glider Wilbur brought from Dayton was left at the freight docks.

"The boat leaked very badly and frequently dipped water, but by constantly bailing we managed to reach the schooner in safety," wrote Wilbur in a journal he kept during the trip. "The strain of rolling and pitching sprang a leak and this, together with what water came over the bow at times, made it necessary to bail frequently."

Wilbur had little experience with boats, but even he could tell that the *Curlicue* was in a serious state of disrepair. "It was in worse condition if possible than the skiff," he reported. "The sails were rotten, the ropes badly worn and the rudder post half-rotted off, and the cabin so dirty and vermin-infested that I kept out of it from first to last."

The weather had been fair with a light wind when the three men set out from Elizabeth City, but it soon deteriorated as the remnants of a hurricane swept through the area. The *Curlicue* sailed downriver after dinner. By the time Perry turned east into the open sound, it was nearly dark. The water in the sound was much rougher, Wilbur noted. The wind increased and shifted to the south, then to the east, making progress in the flat-bottomed schooner difficult. "The waves which were now running quite high struck the boat from below with a heavy shock and threw it back about us as fast as it went forward. The leeway was greater than the headway," he recorded. It took Perry more than four hours to travel less than 12 miles down the Pasquotank River into the sound to North River Point.

As Perry struggled to get the *Curlicue* around the point into calmer waters, the foresail and then the mainsail came loose from the boom and began flapping around, causing the already unstable boat to pitch wildly. Wilbur and the mate had to wrestle both sails onto the deck. By the time Perry set anchor in the North River, all three men were soaked and exhausted. The wind died down overnight, leaving the sound choppy but navigable. After making repairs to the boat and sails, they set off again on Wednesday afternoon.

Perry pulled up to a dock on Kitty Hawk Bay in the dark around 9 p.m. Wilbur stayed on board until Thursday morning. The next morning he went ashore and found a boy, Elijah Baum, playing at the water's edge. He asked the boy to take him to the home of William James Tate.

Chapter Twenty Two

William James Tate at your service

Within minutes of meeting Tate and his wife, Addie, Wilbur was unfolding "a tale of hardship from Elizabeth City to Kitty Hawk, stating he had been some 48 or more hours on the way," Tate later wrote. "[He] told me of how the miserable little boat had to run for harbor in a blow, and how he could not eat the provender cooked by the two men on the boat, and how consequently he had been without food for 48 hours. His account of the trip really amused me. I had heard the same before by others not accustomed to small boats in crossing our North Carolina Sounds. He was a tenderfoot and of course had a tale of woe to tell."[¹]

Tate had invited Wilbur to come to Kitty Hawk. "If you decide to try your machine here and come," Tate wrote, "I will take pleasure in doing all I can for your convenience and success and pleasure, and I assure you you will find a hospitable people when you come among us." Wilbur, it seems, took Tate at his word. He didn't write or wire ahead to announce his intention to accept Tate's invitation; he simply showed up at Tate's front door.

Tate, age 30, and perhaps the best-educated man in Kitty Hawk in 1900, was a second-generation resident. With his wife and their young daughters, Irene and Pauline, he lived in the heart of the "down the road" village about one mile from the boat docks on Kitty Hawk Bay.

His father, William Douglas Tate, had arrived on the Outer Banks aboard the brig *B. M. Prescott*. He was bound for Norfolk, where relatives were already living, but weather kept the ship out of port. Some historians say William Douglas was shipwrecked, but the family insists he deliberately jumped ship with his brother Dan and was rescued from the surf by Kitty Hawk fishermen. William Douglas married and stayed in Kitty Hawk. Dan also stayed in the village and opened a store.

William Douglas died when his son, William James (called Bill by the family), was 11. Bill lived with his Uncle Dan for two years before being sent off to school at the Oxford Orphanage. According to historian

Stephen Kirk, Bill graduated from Atlantic Collegiate Institute in Elizabeth City and then returned to Kitty Hawk. The Tate family, however, is not so sure he actually attended college. In either case, he was still one of the most educated men in the village and his education served him well. He fished, as did most Kitty Hawk men, but in 1900 he was also a county commissioner, notary public and, possibly, the village postmaster. He later served as a lighthouse keeper and a member of the National Aeronautic Association.

Several historians have written that Bill had been postmaster and passed the job on to his wife by the time Wilbur came to the Outer Banks. Tate's descendants disagree. Because Addie had two small children to raise and married women usually did not have careers in those days, it is unlikely that Addie was postmaster, said Suzanne Tate, who researched her in-laws' connections to the first flight for her children's book, *Helping the Wright Brothers*. Bill Tate was the great-uncle of Suzanne's husband, Everett. The family has read that Addie was postmaster, she said, "But they don't believe it." Supporting their belief that she simply helped her husband without formally assuming the job is the 1900 Census: Addie is listed as having no occupation.

Kitty Hawk historian Bill Harris disagrees. It's true that women's lives centered on the home, he said, but women frequently served as postmaster in this part of the country. The job required someone to be available most of the time, but the work was only part-time and could be juggled around a woman's other duties. Most of the men were away from the village, sometimes for long periods of time, either fishing or working for the lifesaving service. Harris's grandmother served as postmaster for 40 years, working from the family store, he pointed out.

The Tates' two-story house was sided with rough, unpainted lumber—standard Outer Banks construction through the 1970s. Part of the downstairs served as the village post office, leaving room for two bedrooms upstairs. Plain and not very large, it was, according to Wilbur, one of the grandest homes in the village.

But when Wilbur arrived on the Tates' doorstep, he was invited in, fed and provided with temporary room and board, even though it meant

Bill and Addie had to move into the bedroom with their children. He settled in, always polite and formal, trying to disrupt their lives as little as possible. His half-built glider arrived by freight boat from Elizabeth City on September 17. According to Tate's account, written some 25 years later, Wilbur immediately set to work on the craft, "sewing, gluing and tying [it] together with string."

The Tate family home in Kitty Hawk, c. 1900
Photo courtesy Grady Tate

"We natives got curious and began to discuss him and his darn fool contraption," Tate recalled. "If comment and criticism had been a helping factor, the Wrights would have flown soon after their arrival at Kitty Hawk."

If Wilbur expected the Tates to house him and his brother for their entire stay, he never said. Dosher had warned Wilbur there were no commercial accommodations in the village. "You will have to bring tents," he wrote. (There was no mention of the many hotels and boarding houses in Nags Head, just 10 miles south, or the many hunt clubs that provided lodging up and down the Currituck Banks—presumably because those areas were unsuitable for flying.) He may have ignored Dosher's warning or thought it unlikely that no rooms were for rent. In any case, sixteen days after Wilbur arrived at Kitty Hawk, Orville joined him at the Tates' home—but Orville came with a tent, cots, coffee, tea, sugar and other camping supplies in hand.

The original plan, according to a letter from Katharine to their father, was that "Orv will go down as soon as Will gets the machine ready." Orville must have been anxious to join his brother. He didn't wait for word that Wilbur had finished the glider but left Dayton on September 24 and arrived five days later—two days faster than Wilbur made the trip.

When Orville arrived, Wilbur was still working on their glider. He had shipped it in pieces: wooden rods, spools of wire, metal fittings and

French sateen for the wing coverings. The design, based on their two seasons of kite experiments in Ohio, called for 18-foot spruce wing spars for which Wilbur shopped in Norfolk. Sixteen-foot lumber was the best he could find. Based on William Tate's recollection of events, the spars were delivered to Kitty Hawk by freight boat two days after Wilbur arrived.

Wilbur had to re-cut and sew the sateen wing covers, which had been made before he left Ohio, to fit the smaller wing design made necessary by the 16-foot wing spars. He borrowed Mrs. Tate's sewing machine and she later said he was as good a seamstress as any she'd seen. In addition to redesigning the wings, Wilbur's progress was slowed by heat and humidity, two elements that take on new meaning for Northerners unaccustomed to summer in the South.

There are differing historical accounts of where Wilbur assembled the glider. Tom Crouch and Stephen Kirk have him working in the Tate's front yard; an earlier biographer, Fred Kelly, writes that the work was done at the site of the brothers' first camp.

Shortly after Orville's arrival, Tate went shopping in Elizabeth City for items the brothers still needed. In his 1928 *Aeronautic Review* article, he recalled that he purchased dishes, an oil stove and gasoline.

Chapter Twenty Three

Camping out

On October 4, the brothers moved into their tent on open sand flats at the edge of Lookout Hill, about a half-mile south of the Tates' home. The camp was primitive, Tate reported, but had everything they needed except a privy and that wasn't necessary, he noted, because "it was only a few yards to the thick copse of bushy undergrowth and hardly any one ever passed that way." Their camping experience in Ohio is unknown, but it's certain that camping on the Outer Banks would have been unlike anything they'd ever experienced before. Indeed, most of their letters home and journal entries made after the trip focus on their living conditions rather than their work with the glider.

The Wrights lived in tents during their first season at Kitty Hawk.
(photo water damaged)
Lib. of Cong., Prints & Photos Div. LC-DIG-pprs-00560v

During this trip, Orville became the brothers' official correspondent, a task he kept for the rest of their partnership. Family members later said it was a job with which he was never comfortable. Wilbur was the better writer of the two, but after this time he wrote only occasional letters to anyone except Octave Chanute, with whom he carried on an active correspondence for several years. Much of what we know about the brothers' first visit to Kitty Hawk comes from Orville's letters. Although in later years they kept detailed daily journals, that wasn't the case on this trip.

In spite of unpredictable winds that kept the glider grounded more often than not, "We have been having a fine time," wrote Orville to Katharine, on October 14. "Altogether we have had the machine out three different days, from two to four hours each time."

After a strong blow a few days earlier, "Kitty Hawkers were out early peering around the edge of the woods and out of their upstairs windows to see whether our camp was still in existence," he wrote. "We were all right, however, and though wind continued up to 30 miles, got the machine out to give it another trial. The wind was too strong and unsteady for us to attempt an ascent in it, so we just flew it like a kite." The wind proved to have the upper hand. After an hour of experimentation, the brothers grounded the glider "kite" for adjustments. The wind promptly picked it back up, carried it 20 feet and crashed it into the sand. "A complete wreck," said Orville. "We dragged the pieces back to camp and began to consider getting home."

Rather than pack up and leave, the brothers repaired the machine and stayed on for another nine days.

The brothers were fascinated by the natural beauty of the Outer Banks. In his October 14 letter, Orville mentioned the same things noted by visitors today: "The sunsets here are the prettiest I have ever seen. The clouds light up in all colors in the background, with deep blue clouds of various shapes fringed with gold before. The moon rises in much the same style, and lights up this pile of sand almost like day."

"But the sand!" he continued. "The sand is the greatest thing in Kitty Hawk, and soon will be the only thing. . . .The sea has washed and the wind blown millions and millions of tons of sand up in heaps along the coast, completely covering houses and forest."

Chapter Twenty Four

Two 'nuts' and the natives

While Orville and Wilbur clearly enjoyed the unfamiliar landscape (in spite of living conditions at camp that were primitive even by Kitty Hawk standards at the time), they grew especially fond of the Outer Bankers who, as Bill Tate had promised, were truly hospitable. Hospitality, however, didn't suspend their disbelief. Tate, along with most other Kitty Hawkers, thought the reason for Wilbur's interest in the Outer Banks crazy. "We were set in our ways," wrote Tate in 1925. "We believed in a good God, a bad Devil, and a hot Hell, and more than anything else we believed that the same good God did not intend man should ever fly." Even so, the "uniform courtesy" of the two brothers to everyone in the village "built up a respect and regard for the two nuts."

John Daniels, another Kitty Hawker who helped the Wrights, recalled, "When they first came down to Kill Devil Hills in the summer of 1900 and begun to experiment with their funny-looking kites we just thought they were a pair of crazy fools. We laughed about 'em among ourselves for a while, but we soon quit laughing and felt sorry for 'em, because they were as nice boys as you'd ever hope to see. . . .They were two of the workingest boys I ever saw, and when they worked *they worked*."

"They were such smart boys—natural-born mechanics—and could do anything they put their hands to," said Daniels in a *Collier's Weekly* interview in 1927. "They built their own camp; they took an old carbide can and made a stove of it; they took a bicycle and geared the thing up so that they could ride it on the sand. They did their own cooking and washing; and they were good cooks too."

"We need no introduction in Kitty Hawk," wrote Orville to Katharine. "Every place we go we are called Mr. Wright. Our fame has spread far and wide up and down the beach." While the brothers enjoyed their notoriety, they were not pretentious and they genuinely enjoyed the people they met and worked with at Kitty Hawk. "Ultimately, it was the

Bankers themselves who most appealed to the Wrights," said their biographer, Tom Crouch. "They were a wild, undisciplined, and self-reliant lot."

Wilbur, writing to his father Milton, said the locals were "friendly and neighborly and I think there is rarely any real suffering among them." "They never have anything good in their lives, and consequently are satisfied with what they have," wrote Orville to Katharine a few weeks later.

Adventurers who observe isolated populations often idealize the hard, simple lives, and the Wrights were no different. Although their remarks seem patronizing today, there's no evidence locals bore them ill will because of their views. The brothers' friendship with Tate lasted their lifetimes and they kept in touch with others, like John Daniels, who played a role in their success.

Chapter Twenty Five

The 1900 glider

Wilbur and Orville finished building their glider shortly after the first of October. It was intended to be flown as a manned kite. The operator

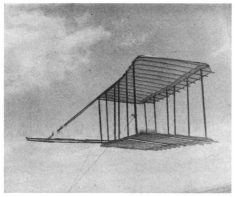

Close-up of the 1901 glider
Lib. of Cong., Prints & Photos Div. LC-DIG-pprs-00555v

was to lie prone across the bottom wing, face forward, in a cradle attached to cables that controlled the warp of both wings. By pushing with his feet, the operator could change the angle of the wings and affect the lateral or side-to-side (yaw and roll) movement of the glider.

The distinctive bi-winged machine—more like a large, ribbed box kite than the Flyer that carried them to fame three years later—had a wingspan of 17 feet 5 inches. The entire assembly weighed less than 50 pounds. The curved upper wing and flat lower wing were about 5 feet across, front to back, and 5 feet apart, top to bottom. The two fabric-covered wings were interconnected with six posts, front and back, for stability and a series of cables connected to the operator cradle which allowed the wings to be warped for directional control. The wings were rigged in a dihedral ("V" shape) angle because design work by previous would-be pilots suggested this provided more lateral stability.

This first glider had no tail. An "elevator" or horizontal rudder stuck out about four feet from the front of the lower wing giving the glider a bird-like appearance. The outstretched operator had to use both hands to grasp this spring-mounted control. In theory, it controlled up-and-down movement (pitch) by being raised or lowered. The front design provided erratic control; later gliders would incorporate a tail rudder that worked much better.

Chapter Twenty Six

Wing-warping

Orville and Wilbur believed they succeeded in powered flight because first they spent time learning to fly without power. They spent years flying ordinary kites, then larger unmanned and manned gliders, studying aerodynamics and figuring out how to control their gliders in the air.

It's also good to remember the old adage, "You can't see the forest for the trees," when thinking about the Wrights' success. Wilbur, in particular, was able to strip problems down to their bare bones. He was a methodical thinker. He started at the beginning, charting his course, taking into consideration what others might have done but unwilling to put much trust in anything he hadn't done for himself.

Others pursuing the secret of powered flight at the end of the 19th century accepted that man could launch himself into the air and stay there if the winds allowed. Many jumped right to the power part, spending little or no time trying to learn how man could ride those winds once he was up in the air. They assumed that *power* in and of itself was all they needed.

That assumption killed many of them.

Wilbur looked at their work, studied what they did, how they did it, and tried to understand where they went wrong. From his vantage point, he began to believe that power wasn't all it had been cracked up to be: Control was what fliers needed first and foremost. And so control was what he and Orville set out to invent.

Orville, writing in 1920, told how the two brothers had a long interest in flying, but their efforts were spurred by a book they read in 1899 on ornithology. "We could not understand that there was anything about a bird that would enable it to fly that could not be built on a larger scale and used by man," he wrote. "At this time our thought pertained more to gliding flight and soaring."

After researching material suggested by the Smithsonian Institution, "we became highly enthusiastic with the idea of gliding as a sport," said Orville, but they wanted to know why Lilienthal and Pilcher—two well-known would-be aviators who focused on gliding—crashed and died. "We found that both of these experimenters had attempted to maintain balance merely by the shifting of the weight of their bodies. . . . We at once set to work to devise a more efficient means of maintaining the equilibrium."

Wilbur looked to birds for an answer. He believed they controlled their movements, in part, by altering the aerodynamic characteristics of the wings. "The thought came to me that possibly it adjusted the tips of its wings . . . so as to present one tip at a positive angle and the other as a negative angle . . . turning itself into an animated windmill," explained Wilbur later. "When its body had revolved . . . as far as it wished, it reversed the process and started turning the other way. The balance was controlled by utilizing dynamic reactions of the air instead of shifting weight."

Once he understood the "why," Wilbur had to figure out the "how." The solution occurred to him one afternoon as he twisted a long inner-tube box in his bicycle shop. "Twisting . . . that was the answer," explains Crouch in *The Bishop's Boys*. "Rather than treating each wingtip as an independent unit, he would throw a complete helical twist across the entire wing structure in either direction." This concept, said Wilbur, "was the silent birth of all that underlies human flight."

When Wilbur Wright figured out that simple movement offsetting the positive angle shift of one airplane wing with a corresponding negative angle shift of the other wing, he unlocked the secret of controlled flight. It was the one thing aviation greats who tried to fly before 1903 never understood.

In later years trying to secure and protect their patents, there was much controversy about this "wing-warping" business. The Wright brothers claimed to be the first to use it by creating a system of pulleys and cables that flexed the wings of a plane. It put the onus of re-creating the center of gravity on the machine itself, guided by a simple controlled movement on the part of the pilot in response to wind changes. The wing-warping control for their first gliders was located at the pilot's feet; by 1902 they had designed a cradle that allowed the pilot to move the wings simply by flexing his hips.

Orville explained the need for lateral control in an address to the Franklin Institute in Philadelphia in 1914: "If the center of support of an aeroplane surface would remain fixed at one point . . . equilibrium would be a simple matter. But the location of the center of pressure on an aeroplane surface changes with every change in the angle at which the air strikes the surface."

Octave Chanute, according to Crouch, coined the term wing-warping after Wilbur first explained it to him, but he may have never clearly understood the concept. Although he urged the brothers to patent their invention, he later said he was referring only to the mechanics of concept. He insisted earlier aviation experimenters had just as much claim to the idea of flexing wings as the Wright brothers. "[Chanute] saw the Wrights as extraordinarily gifted mechanics who had put old ideas into new bottles," wrote Crouch. "Their genius . . . was to be found in an ability to make other men's ideas work." In retrospect, most historians believe he was uncharacteristically short-sighted on this subject.

In addition to Chanute's claims that the Wright brothers' patent gave them too much credit, other aviators stepped forward to claim the use of wing-warping in glider designs in the 1880s. Eventually, these claims were unsuccessful, and the Wrights retained credit for developing wing-warping as the key to controlled flight.

"It is rather amusing . . . to find now that people knew exactly how to fly all the time," wrote Wilbur in 1912. "After the real truth had been discovered, the old experiments seemed to have an importance in value sometimes which they did not have at the time."

Chapter Twenty Seven

Getting down to work

Wilbur considered his trip to Kitty Hawk a working vacation. "I have not taken up the problem [of flying] with the expectation of financial profit. Neither do I have any strong expectation of achieving the solution at the present time or possibly any time," he wrote to his father shortly after arriving at Kitty Hawk. "My trip would be no great disappointment if I accomplished practically nothing. I look upon it as a pleasure at the same cost."

In the same letter, he explained the work at hand. "I have my machine nearly finished. It is not to have a motor and is not expected to fly in any true sense of the word. My idea is merely to experiment and practice with a view to solving the problem of equilibrium. I have plans which I hope to find much in advance of the methods tried by previous experimenters."

In spite of their plans to keep the glider in the air for hours each day, by October 10 they had been able to fly it as a kite only three times.

Only once in those first days—possibly the first day they put the glider up, according to Crouch—had the wind been strong enough to allow Wilbur to climb aboard and climb to a height of about 15 feet while Orville and Bill Tate held lines and flew the machine like a kite. Within seconds the glider was bucking to and fro and Wilbur was yelling, "Let me down!"

According to the Wrights' calculations, winds of 10 to 20 mph were needed to conduct their unmanned experiments. Sustained winds of about 25 mph were necessary to keep a manned glider aloft. They had chosen Kitty Hawk, in part, because what they were told about wind speeds on the Outer Banks seemed to meet their requirements. Although the September average, according to weather bureau records, was just over 13 mph, data showed considerably higher winds on several days. Tate had also written that winds "are always steady, generally from 10 to 20 miles velocity per hour." But they soon found out the wind at Kitty Hawk was far from what they expected. Light breezes alternated with gale force blows, neither suitable for gliding. Only a few of their 40 days at Kitty Hawk that year offered the wind speeds needed for their planned experiments. Instead of the hours of personal flight time the brothers expected to log over their stay, Wilbur spent less than 10 minutes in the air while Orville remained earthbound.

But the Wright brothers excelled at improvisation and invention. "Suitable winds not being plentiful," wrote Orville in an article for *Century* magazine in 1908, "we found it necessary, in order to test the new balancing system, to fly the machine as a kite without a man on board, operating the levers through cords from the ground. This did not give the practice anticipated, but it inspired confidence in the new system of balance." They systematically tested their rudimentary glider under a variety of conditions. The brothers loaded chains of varying weights onto the cradle and flew the thing like a kite with strings attached to the rudder, noting wind speeds and observing drag and lift.

Not all the flights were unmanned. In addition to Wilbur's brief flight early in the month, Tom Tate, a local 12-year-old, went up on the kite several times one day in mid-October. On October 19, winds were high enough to allow Wilbur to fly again. He made several glides, some 300 to 400 feet long lasting up to 15 seconds. He later estimated he spent close to two minutes actually "flying." It doesn't sound like much today, but in 1900 it was something few men had experienced. It was time enough to confirm that wind wasn't their only problem. A more serious concern was lift: the glider's ability to rise while moving forward in the wind.

Young Tom Tate, Dan Tate's son and Bill Tate's nephew, flew on the Wrights' glider in 1900.
Lib. of Cong., Prints & Photos Div.
LC-DIG-pprs-00545v

The planned purpose of their Kitty Hawk experiments this year was to test what they believed to be a better idea for controlling a flying machine. On this count, the trip was a success: Their wing-warping system worked. But flying was a complicated process, filled with trial-and-error. Not all their "better" ideas worked.

Without power, launching the glider was problematic. In Wilbur's first letter to Octave Chanute, dated May 13, 1900, he told of his plan to build a 150-foot tower. The tower would have a pulley at the top and a counter-weighted rope threaded through the pulley would be attached to the glider, he explained. "The wind will blow the machine out from the base of the tower and the weight will be sustained partly by the upward pull of the rope and partly by the lift of the wind." This idea would allow the brothers to stay in the air for hours at a time, getting a "maximum of practice with a minimum of effort," as Orville later put it.

Chanute discouraged the idea as "dangerous." Wilbur forged ahead with the tower anyway, although for some reason he scaled it down. Measurements for the structure are unavailable but given the limitations of material and tools, it was probably little more than 10 or 20 feet tall.

Orville described the launching procedure they used to their sister, Katharine, in a letter written from Kitty Hawk on October 14, 1900: "Well, after erecting a derrick from which to swing our rope with which we fly the machine, we sent it up about 20 feet, at which height we attempt to keep it by the manipulation of the strings to the rudder. The greatest difficulty is in keeping it down. It naturally wants to go higher and higher." Pulling the glider down caused it to make "a terrific dart for the ground," he wrote.

The derrick proved an unwieldy system of control, and they realized putting themselves in the air by this method would be a serious accident waiting to happen the first time the wind died unexpectedly. After using it for unmanned experiments on October 10, they followed the advice of Chanute and the example of Otto Lilienthal, both of whom preferred launching from sand hills.

By the time Orville and Wilbur headed back to Dayton, on October 23, they knew they were on the right track. At the same time, they knew their glider design needed modification. The dihedral design proved too vulnerable to side winds. The wing span, reduced at the last minute because Wilbur couldn't find suitable lumber in Norfolk, had to be longer. They needed to improve the simultaneous operation of the wing-warping cradle and elevator. And they had to figure out why the machine's lift fell considerably short of their calculations.

"Although we were highly pleased with the performance of the machine, in so far as lateral control was concerned, we were disappointed with its lifting ability. We did not know whether its failure to lift according to the calculations made previous to our going to Kitty Hawk was due to the construction of our machine, or whether the tables of air pressure, at that time generally accepted, were incorrect," wrote Orville in *How We Invented the Airplane*. "There was another year coming and we weren't discouraged. We had just begun."

Back to the Outer Banks, 1901

Tom Tate in front of camp building at Kitty Hawk, 1901
Lib. of Cong., Prints & Photos Div. LC-DIG-pprs-00700v

Chapter Twenty Eight

Regrouping in Dayton

By the time Wilbur and Orville headed back to Dayton in October, 1900, they had already begun designing a bigger, better machine. The first glider, estimated to have cost about $15, patched and held together with splints, was of no use to them. Before they left Kitty Hawk, according to biographer Tom Crouch, they "carried the machine back down the trail going south out of town and gave it one last toss from the top of a dune. It came to rest in a sandy hollow." Locals salvaged what they could of the materials. Addie Tate sewed dresses for her daughters from the sateen fabric covering the wings. The last unclaimed piece of the machine disappeared during a gale the following July.

Although their experiments had proved useful, the 1900 glider's instability had forced them to settle for flying it like a kite, adding an occasional sand bag—or a local boy—for weight. It was also undersized for carrying a full-grown man. In 1901, they intended to fix these problems and spend more time in the air themselves. The brothers had the design for a new machine completed in May.

For a machine to fly, it must have lift, something defined as the aerodynamic force working against the force of gravity and perpendicular to the relative wind, causing an airfoil (wing) to rise. To have lift, equilibrium must exist between the weight of the machine, the wind speed and the total wing surface. The lighter the wind or the heavier the machine, the more wing surface it must have to get off the ground.

When designing the first glider, the Wrights counted on winds of 10 to 20 mph, wind speeds both the weather bureau and Tate had assured them were probable. What they got was considerably different: One day the winds would barely blow, too light to give the 1900 glider enough lift to fly; the next day they'd roar across the dunes at gale force, sending the machine out of control.

The Wrights designed their 1900 machine with 225 square feet of wing but cut back to 165 square feet when Wilbur was unable to buy sufficiently long timbers. The 1901 machine had 2.5 times the surface area with a 22-foot wingspan (the 1900 machine was just under 17.5 feet).

The new glider was the largest ever flown by anyone, anywhere.

Another part of the lift equation is determined by the shape of the wing. Effective wings—whether they be on birds or on airplanes—are not perfectly flat. The leading edge is curved, and they are attached to the body at an angle so that the trailing edge of the wing is lower than the leading edge.

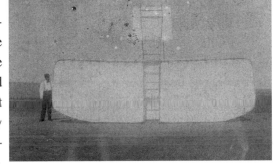

The Wrights used a relatively flat curve on the wings of the 1900 plane even though they based their calculations on lift and drag tables prepared by Otto Lilienthal whose glider wings had a much smaller arc. In 1901, they followed Lilienthal's measurements exactly although they had begun to suspect his tables contained

Orville with the 1901 glider
Lib. of Cong., Prints & Photos Div. LC-DIG-pprs-00574v

substantial errors. It was almost unthinkable: No aviation engineer had yet questioned Lilienthal's calculations or tried to duplicate his measurements. Octave Chanute used Lilienthal, Samuel Langley used Lilienthal. Who were the Wrights—two bicycle mechanics without high school diplomas or formal engineering educations—to question his work?

In Orville's own words: "In order to satisfy our own minds . . . we undertook a number of experiments to determine the comparative lifting qualities of planes as compared with curved surfaces. . . . The experiments were so crudely carried out that close measurements were not possible. But the results of these experiments confirmed us in the belief already formed that the accepted tables of air pressure were not to be altogether relied upon."

Even so, when Chanute, their mentor, pointed out that their glider hadn't met Lilienthal's standards for wing curvature or surface square footage, they set out to build another glider that would. It was one of the few instances when the brothers deferred to accepted science and didn't follow their own instincts.

But the brothers didn't defer to their predecessors in flight on every front. They included a moveable front elevator for controlling horizontal stability as they had on their 1900 machine. And they persisted in using a prone pilot position, which reduced drag and allowed the pilot to operate a wing-warping cradle with his feet. Lilienthal, Chanute and other aviation pioneers had favored keeping the operator upright, dangling from the wings, because they perceived this position to be safer. Crashes and operator deaths had proved this method—which relied on shifting the weight of the operator from one side to the other for lateral control—didn't work very well.

Chapter Twenty Nine

Unwanted help

Wilbur and Orville Wright preferred to work alone. They had worked successfully as a two-man team since their teens—publishing several newspapers and running printing and bicycle shops—and saw no reason to change that habit. Their father, Milton, cautioned his children to remember blood was always thicker than water. It was a lesson the Wrights took to heart: Only occasionally were others (almost always friends) brought into their business ventures.

In the spring of 1901, when Chanute suggested to the Wrights that he send George Spratt and Edward Huffaker to help them at Kitty Hawk, the brothers weren't particularly happy. Chanute, expecting resistance, explained that Huffaker would bring his own glider, built at Chanute's request, and that he and Spratt would conduct their own experiments as well. "If Chanute was honestly asking for their assistance in testing his craft and training his people, [the Wrights] could not easily refuse," wrote Crouch in *The Bishop's Boys*.

And so the Wrights left Dayton for the Outer Banks on July 7, not keen on the company they would be hosting at Kitty Hawk but anxious to start work. This was the only year they would come to the Outer Banks to conduct flight experiments during the summer. The timing of their first trip had been dictated by their bicycle business: In Dayton, fall months were the slowest. Stephen Kirk, in his book *First in Flight*, said the Wrights made their 1901 trip to the Outer Banks nearly two months earlier than planned to take advantage of the "ideal time of year for experimenting." It seems more likely, however, that enthusiasm for their new hobby was what dictated the early July arrival. Any local would have told them that summer offered less wind, higher humidity and oppressive heat —hardly ideal conditions for their work.

In either case, Wilbur and Orville were able to leave the bicycle shop in the hands of their old friend and newly hired mechanic, Charlie Taylor, and travel together. They took the train, as they did in 1900, to Hampton

Roads and then the ferry to Norfolk, where they boarded another train for Elizabeth City. A severe storm delayed their departure. On July 10, they traveled by private boat to Kitty Hawk. After spending the first night with Bill Tate, they set out to build a camp some four miles from the village at the base of Kill Devil Hill. The location's big hills and expansive sand flats better suited their purposes. This year they erected tents for sleeping and eating but built a wood shelter for the glider with lumber ordered in Elizabeth City.

In 1901, Kill Devil Hill and the new camp—located roughly mid-island between the sound and the ocean on one of the wider stretches of barrier island—were probably south of the Currituck County line, according to sources at the Outer Banks History Center and the National Park Service. The Wrights themselves referred to the area as Dare County. It should be noted, however, that there has been an ongoing dispute about the southern boundary of Atlantic Township (the part of Currituck County transferred to Dare county in 1920) and

View from the top of Kill Devil Hill
Lib. of Cong., Prints & Photos Div. LC-DIG-pprs-00545v

some local historians still believe all the Wrights' North Carolina flights took place in Currituck.

Two of the Outer Banks' 11 lifesaving stations, Kitty Hawk and Kill Devil Hills, were less than five miles away, although five miles was a considerable trek through soft sand. Men from the Kitty Hawk lifesaving crew had occasionally helped the Wrights in 1900 and they, in turn, took photographs of the crew and the station house. Joe Dosher, the U.S. Weather Bureau employee who first responded to Wilbur's inquiry about the Outer Banks weather, worked in a small shack next door to the Kitty

Hawk station. He had loaned them his wind anemometer for their experiments that year.

During the Wrights' stay in 1901, the stations would have been closed because they were manned only from September through April. Had the brothers needed help, they probably could have gotten it: Most of the lifesavers lived in or near Kitty Hawk all year, fishing and farming in the off-season or providing services for summer residents and tourists at Nags Head. But this year, the Wrights were better equipped and less dependent on the village. They would have all the outside help they needed with Huffaker, Spratt and, for a few days, Chanute, the most respected aeronautical engineer of their day.

Chapter Thirty

From bad to worse

Things got off to a bad start. Rainy weather followed by typical mid-summer heat and hordes of mosquitoes delayed getting their camp in order and, consequently, their glider experiments. Lack of fresh water at their camp site added to their misery. Spratt arrived about a week after the Wrights; Huffaker showed up a week later. By July 25, Huffaker's glider—an impossible design of cardboard tubing and fabric—was assembled and quickly abandoned after it failed to go airborne. The Wrights' glider was completed on July 26 and put into the air for the first time the next day.

As Orville recalled years later, "This machine was tested a number of times in free gliding flight and also as a kite. In the gliding flights the fore-and-aft stability or control of the machine did not seem to be as good as that of the previous year." They also determined this new glider lacked the aerodynamic efficiency of their 1900 machine. They confirmed their own belief that too much curvature in an aircraft wing was as bad as none at all. Flatter wings may not have met Lilienthal's standards, but they were definitely more stable. They redesigned the curvature of the wings, then flew the machine as a kite, taking measurements of lift and drift. As in 1900, their own calculations varied significantly from the airfoil data published more than ten years earlier by Lilienthal. They continued to fiddle with the wings, flying the machine and taking measurements after each adjustment. They eventually amassed data from several hundred flights, several exceeding 300 feet. They couldn't seem to improve the stability of the glider. Stalling was a major problem.

"The machine refused to act like our machine last year and at times seemed to be entirely beyond our control," wrote Orville to Katharine on July 28. "On the occasion, it began gliding higher and higher (Will doing the gliding) until it finally came almost at a stop. . . . This was precisely the fix Lilienthal got into when he was killed." In Lilienthal's case, the glider dropped straight to the ground and broke his neck. The Wrights had studied Lilienthal's accident and added a front elevator to their design which proved effective. "This wound up in the most encouraging performance of the whole afternoon," Orville explained. "Our machine made a flat descent to the ground with no injury to either operator or machine."

Wilbur viewed this "encouraging performance" as one of only a few successes in their experiments that summer. His diary reflected his growing disappointment: "Our hopes of obtaining actual practice in the air are decreased to about one fifth of what we hoped. Five minutes in free flight is a good day's record. We have not yet reached so good an average as this."

There was never better proof of the disparity in the visions of creative minds than at Kitty Hawk that summer. Huffaker and Spratt viewed the Wrights' experiments as successful. Huffaker, a former associate of

Samuel Langley's, was especially enthusiastic. In the diaries he kept for Chanute, Huffaker pronounced several days' work as "good" and "excellent." Not only was the 1901 glider larger than any other successfully flown, but it also broke all known

Octave Chanute, Orville, and Edward Huffaker at the 1901 camp
Lib. of Cong., Prints & Photos Div. LC-DIG-pprs-00581v

records for distance traveled on several occasions. Chanute, who arrived on August 4 and stayed for six days, told Wilbur he believed their results to be "better than had ever before been attained." He wrote to Wilbur after leaving Kitty Hawk, "I think you have performed quite an achievement in sailing with surfaces wider than any which I dared to use. . . . " He considered their work successful enough to urge Wilbur to address the Western Society of Engineers, the most prestigious American group interested in promoting controlled, manned flight.

Exactly what Chanute did during his stay on the Outer Banks is not clear. At 69 years old, he was too old to assist in any of the hard, physical labor of handling and launching the glider. He did bring a camera and take 12 pictures although most did not turn out (a common problem in the early days of photography). Chanute also took his own notes and made some measurements during the experiments he observed, but he was unable to assist the Wrights in solving their problems. After analyzing data from one of the Wrights' glides, he admitted he was puzzled. "I have tried to figure out this glide with the Lilienthal coefficients, but they do not fit at all," he wrote to Wilbur in September.

Neither brother was happy with their second trip to Kitty Hawk. In addition to their experimental failures, their stay was marked with miserable weather, swarms of mosquitoes, and the unpleasant company of Huffaker, whom they found to be lazy and slobbish. To make matters worse, by the time they left, Wilbur was sick with a bad cold. They had planned to stay longer but "It rained four days in succession after you left and then blew straight from the south till our departure," explained Wilbur in a letter to Chanute. "We saw it as a waste of time to attempt to do anything at this season of the year."

"The boys walked in unexpectedly on Thursday morning," Katharine, wrote to their father in late August. "[They] haven't had much to say about flying. They can only talk about how disagreeable Huffaker was."

"We doubted that we would ever resume our experiments," wrote Wilbur several years later. ". . . When we looked at the time and money which we expended, and considered the progress made and the distance yet to go, we considered our experiments a failure. At this time I made the prediction that men would sometime fly, but that it would not be within our lifetime." On the train ride home, Orville said, Wilbur lamented that "not within a thousand years would man ever fly."

These long-after-the-fact comments, while widely reported and taken as proof Wilbur was about to give up his quest, are likely distorted memories. At the time, Wilbur expressed disappointment—but never such pessimism—over the summer's work. Wilbur and Chanute exchanged sev - eral letters in late August. None came close to suggesting Wilbur thought successful flight was beyond his reach. In a letter to Chanute dated August 29, Wilbur sent several pages of lift, drift and resistance data recorded during the previous month's glides. He annotated the measurements with his own theories about what the data means and how it could be used—hardly the work of someone convinced his effort was wasted.

That summer, Orville never directly commented on his thoughts about their chances for success so it's impossible to know if he shared the profound sense of failure attributed to Wilbur. Several years later, Orville wrote: "Our experiments of 1901 were rather discouraging to us because we felt that they had demonstrated that some of the most firmly established laws . . . were mostly, if not entirely, incorrect. At first we had taken up the problem merely as a matter of sport, but now it was apparent that if we were to make much progress it would be necessary to get better tables from which to make our calculations." At the time, Orville was only commenting on their battles with mosquitoes, their methods for washing dishes without water and other colorful—but strictly social—events. It is clear his was a supporting role. Wilbur was making the decisions, documenting the work and flying the gliders. Most historians believe, in 1901, the quest to fly was still Wilbur's not Orville's. There's no indication that Orville shared his brother's passionate belief that flight was possible, or that he would have pursued the problem of manned flight on his own.

Chapter Thirty One

Raising questions

Wilbur and Orville Wright left the Outer Banks in the fall of 1901 discouraged, unsure if they would return. Their glider, designed so carefully to conform to the accepted aeronautical data available for lift and air pressures, didn't fly right. They left it behind, parked in the wooden garage they had built at the beginning of their visit.

For more than 10 years, experimenters with aircraft had relied on tables of air pressure published by the German aviator, Otto Lilienthal, in 1889. Lilienthal's data was used to calculate how much speed and wind were required to lift machines with various weights and wingspans off the ground and into sustained flight. The Wrights relied on his data during their first two years of flying experiments.

Once a flying machine was in the air, controlling flight was also dependent upon Lilienthal's data. Few aviation experimenters had given control much thought, but the Wrights wanted to understand how a machine turned and behaved in the air. To have control, they needed to know how air pressure affected their machine. From the onset of their flying experiments, the Wrights maintained that control would be the key to powered flight. Their experience in 1900 convinced them they understood control.

A side view of the 1901 glider being flown as a kite
Lib. of Cong., Prints & Photos Div.
LC-DIG-pprs-00580v

Even so, the 1900 glider didn't fly according to their theoretical calculations. They suspected Lilienthal's data was wrong but decided, instead, the problem lay in their own design. They had built their glider wings with less curvature than Lilienthal used in making his calculations. And quite possibly the curve of the wing made a substantial difference.

No one really knew for sure.

So in 1901, the Wrights designed their wings to more closely match Lilienthal's, but the glider was larger than any other ever flown up until that time. In its first trials, it nosedived or stalled repeatedly. "The stability or control of the machine did not seem to be as good as that of the previous year," wrote Orville some years later of their experience with an "improved" glider at Kitty Hawk in 1901.

The brothers first decided their new curved wing design—a design encouraged by Chanute—was causing the problem. Some of the problems were solved in the field. The glider's penchant for unpredictable nosedives was reduced with adjustments to the wing shape and the front elevator. The Wrights, however, were not content to make design changes without understanding the science that made them necessary. In Wilbur's mind, particularly, trial-and-error achievement without the support of solid theory was failure.

Then there was the problem of inadequate lift. The wings provided only one-third of the predicted lift requiring either higher winds or a lighter load in order to stay aloft. No amount of fiddling in the field fixed this problem. The glider simply wouldn't get off the ground and stay in the air at the wind speed and with the weight calculated from Lilienthal's aeronautical tables.

The formula for calculating lift required multiplying a constant air pressure coefficient with the total surface area of the machine, the total velocity of the machine squared, and another coefficient based on the shape and angle of the airfoil ($L = k \times S \times V^2 \times C_1$). "A number of measurements were made of the machine flown as a kite to determine the lift and the drift as various angles of incidence. The results obtained did not agree at all with the estimated values computed from Lilienthal and other accepted tables of air pressure," said Orville.

Always intrigued by the minutiae of the engineering problems they tackled, the brothers documented hundreds of flights that summer, recording wind velocity, angle of incidence (the angle at which the wing surface and air stream meet), lift (the pounds of aerodynamic force exerted upward on the aircraft perpendicular to the wind) and drift (drag). It was the first time such extensive data had been collected using a full-size flying machine, and the data suggested Lilienthal's numbers were wrong.

Lilienthal wasn't the only sticking point in available aviation science. Accepted theory held that the center of air pressure always moved forward as the angle of a wing meeting the air stream decreased. Edward Huffaker and George Spratt, who worked with the Wrights at Kitty Hawk in 1901, were skeptical. At their urging, the Wrights tested the theory that summer with a kite and agreed that under some conditions the center of pressure appeared to move backward.

Both of these discoveries were crucial to the Wrights' eventual success but neither brother realized it at the time. They went home to Dayton, believing their experiments that summer were failures.

Chanute, with whom Wilbur kept up a lively correspondence during their first years of friendship, sensed Wilbur's despair. He also recognized the Wrights had made more progress than any of their contemporaries. No one had ever successfully flown a glider as large as theirs—and no one seemed to have as good a grasp on the issues of control. Just about anyone else who'd made notable progress in flight—Lilienthal included —had been killed by their inability to control their machines. The Wrights put their glider into the air and lived to tell about it. Chanute encouraged them not to give up.

But it was to be their failures that summer that led ultimately to their success. The year before, Wilbur had suggested to Chanute that the tables of air pressure prepared by Lilienthal and used by aeronautical engineers of their day might be incorrect. Chanute had dismissed the possibility. Now Wilbur was fairly certain the data was wrong. He exchanged weekly letters with Chanute, arguing Lilienthal's tables were wrong. In one letter, Wilbur recounted the documentation of one Lilienthal glide to Chanute and then asked incredulously, "Did [Lilienthal] find in actual practice that so slight an increase of speed almost doubled the length of his glides?" The answer was, of course, probably not. Wilbur also criticized Lilienthal's numbers in a speech he made before the Western Society of Engineers in Chicago on September 18. After being inundated with Wilbur's data from the 1901 experiments and his subsequent calculations, Chanute finally began to encourage his questions.

To be fair to Lilienthal, it should be pointed out that he relied upon an accepted coefficient for air pressure that was developed in the mid-1700s by John Smeaton, one of the world's first professional engineers. Lilienthal's calculations were correct; it was the Smeaton coefficient the Wrights proved faulty.

Smeaton, an Englishman, made numerous contributions to engineering science. He invented hydraulic cement and built the first all-masonry lighthouse on a rock in open seas. He designed better canals and bridges and improved the steam engine. It was his interest in windmills and waterwheels that led to his connection with the Wright brothers. His infamous calculation (of which most biographical sketches make no mention) was included in an addendum to a gold medal winning report given to the British Royal Society in 1759. That error aside, the report, "An experimental enquiry concerning the natural powers of wind and water to turn mills, and other machines, depending on a circular motion," is considered one of the greatest contributions to engineering in the 18th century.

Smeaton wasn't expecting folks using his coefficient to fly, but fellow Englishman George Cayley used it anyway in designing a glider. Presumably because Cayley's gliders did fly, future aeronauts used the same resource for their own calculations. The fact was, under some circumstances, the coefficient, .005, was correct. Under other circumstances, it was too high by as much as 40 percent. The Wrights gauged .0033 to be a better number—not much, really, when you consider the state of mathematical calculations before the 20th century. But when Wilbur and Orville multiplied out the formula for calculating lift for a full-size glider, it translated into a need for up to 10 mph more wind speed in order to conduct their planned tests at Kitty Hawk. And that was significant.

Chapter Thirty Two

Finding answers

The brothers began testing small wing-shaped pieces of steel sheeting (airfoils) mounted on a freestanding bicycle wheel laid horizontally and exposed to natural wind. In this case, in addition to adapting bicycle parts, they also relied on bicycle power. When natural wind proved insufficient for their work, they mounted the test wheel horizontally above the front tire of one of their bicycles and pedaled down the street.

These airfoils, one flat and one cambered, were set at angles on the wheel which, according to Lilienthal's tables, should have balanced each other, keeping the wheel motionless. The balance wasn't there; the tables were wrong. They abandoned the bicycle and began building a wind tunnel to compile their own data.

It was just the sort of investigation the brothers loved to undertake. They often immersed themselves in subjects that caught their fancy. Reading dozens of books on a single subject, spending days collecting data and weeks recalculating equations to achieve some scientific purpose—activities which might sound like work to some people—represented fun to the Wrights.

One of the remarkable things about the Wright brothers' quest to fly is the small amount of money invested in their success. While other men were spending thousands of dollars on elaborate models, finely calibrated testing devices, specially engineered launching equipment, and salaries for numerous assistants, Orville and Wilbur did the work themselves, largely with materials at hand.

The Wrights' first glider cost just $15. By the end of 1901, including the cost of their trips to Kitty Hawk, they had spent less than $300 on this new pastime. Samuel Langley, the most prominent American pursuing powered flight in the late 19th century, went through more than $50,000 with far less promising results.

Money wasn't the only difference between Langley and the Wrights' approach to solving the problem of flight. Although Langley was largely self-taught, as were the Wrights, he had achieved academic standing as a professor of physics and Secretary of the Smithsonian Institution. In 1891, he had published *Experiments in Aerodynamics*, but the data presented in the book proved unreliable. "Many of his conclusions [were] little better than guesswork," wrote Orville some years later.

In fact, Langley showed little interest in understanding the principles behind flight. Rather than trying to learn why and how things flew, he focused on the machines themselves using trial-and-error to modify designs on hundreds of models.

The Wrights, on the other hand, became caught up in the science of flight. They believed in mathematical preciseness; they knew good science should be predictable. Wright biographer Tom Crouch did a good job of summing up their attitude when he wrote: "Wilbur and Orville had a low tolerance for guesswork." In an article published in *Century* magazine in 1908, Orville wrote: "We had taken up aeronautics merely as sport. We reluctantly entered upon the scientific side of it. But we soon found the work so fascinating that we were drawn into it deeper and deeper."

By this time the brothers were making a point of publicly not taking individual credit for their work. However, from correspondence and other accountings by the Wrights, it's clear that their individual talents meshed perfectly—and separately—to solve this dilemma: Wilbur worked out the mathematical proofs while Orville started the process of discovery by devising an experiment translating Wilbur's calculations into visual evidence.

Orville began with an old starch box about 18 inches long, according to Phil Scott, author of *The Shoulders of Giants* . "[He] cut a hole in it for a glass window, then inside he placed a surface cambered 1 to 12 like [Otto] Lilienthal's, balanced it against a flat plate of equal area, and with a fan blew a stream of air into the box."

"After just one day he could tell for sure something was off with the Lilienthal tables," reported Scott. From the starch box, experiments progressed to airfoils mounted on a bicycle tire rim. When those experiments provided encouraging but less-than-precise results, the brothers set about building a wind tunnel.

Wind tunnels used to study aerodynamics today are often room-sized machines powered by computer-driven engines. Though the "tunnel" itself may be no more than a plywood box, the sensors and imaging equipment are sophisticated and high-tech, generating detailed graphs and maps of air flow, air pressures and air resistance in a matter of minutes. In 1901, wind tunnel technology was barely a quarter-century old.

Much of what the Wrights knew about building wind tunnels was gleaned that summer from Spratt. Although his own wind tunnel experiments had been unsuccessful, Spratt explained what he'd done and how he'd done it. The testing device needed to do more than simply measure lift or drag as previous wind tunnel experiments did, he said. To provide data really useful in designing flying machines, the device should balance the two forces against each other. The Wrights remembered his advice. Their first tunnel was built in a matter of hours of shop discards and spare materials. Less a tunnel than a wooden trough with a fan at one end, it used tiny balances set on a measuring platform less than one foot square. The fan was driven by a one-horse, gas-powered motor borrowed from the bicycle shop.

"The results obtained, with the rough apparatus used, were so interesting in their nature, and gave evidence of such possibility of exactness in measuring the value (of air pressures), that we decided to construct an apparatus specially for making tables giving the value of (pressures) at all angles up to 30 degrees and for surfaces of different curvatures and different relative lengths and breadths," wrote Wilbur to Chanute in early October.

After testing Lilienthal's data with their smaller wind tunnels, the brothers built a larger tunnel, 6 feet long and 16 inches square. A metal hood shielded a fan at one end while a glass plate in the top of the box allowed them to view the experiment without interfering with air flow. The fan, driven by an old gearbox, produced an average wind speed of 27 mph at 4,000 rpm, according to Crouch.

They constructed two balances for the tunnel—one that measured lift and one that measured the lift-to-drag ratio—from old hacksaw blades and bicycle spokes. Orville cut and hammered more than 50 different air-foils to 1/32 of an inch thick, most from scrap pieces of 20-gauge sheet metal. Some of the airfoils were flat, some curved. Most were rectangular but some were square and a few had rounded corners. The area of each was about 6 square inches.

The brothers spent several weeks making thousands of measurements, using the various airfoils in a constant wind. Each of the airfoils was tested at 14 different angles for lift and 12 different angles for lift-to-drift ratio.

The airfoil tests proved that Lilienthal's tables based on Smeaton's coefficient were wrong. His numbers for the lift coefficient (C_L) also proved to be inaccurate, a mistake Wilbur attributed to Lilienthal's home-made anemometer (a machine that measured wind speed) which used the Smeaton coefficient in its calibrations. In any case, the accuracy of instruments in 1900 was highly suspect. Wilbur found readings on his own anemometers varied by as much as 10 percent.

Wilbur also questioned how Lilienthal applied some of his data. Rather than taking the thousands of readings required to test various air-foil shapes under different wind conditions, Lilienthal extrapolated his limited test data, making assumptions about the performance of air pressure on airfoils that the Wrights proved inaccurate.

Lilienthal's erroneous data caused Orville and Wilbur extra work and frustration, but the brothers never had harsh words for the man whose death in a glider accident served as their inspiration to fly. "I have read the Lilienthal translation," Wilbur wrote to Chanute in November, 1901. "The more it is studied the more wonderful it becomes. Although, as I see it, errors are not entirely absent, yet considering that it was a pioneer work, developing an entirely new field, it is remarkably sound and accurate. . . . His errors, on the whole, are so small compared with his truth that his book must be considered an extraordinary one to be the work of a single man." Lilienthal remained their inspiration.

There was no grumbling about missed opportunities or wasted time. The Wrights must have realized the wind tunnel tests provided them with far more than they set out to gain. It was the zenith of their partnership:

At no other time would their different abilities be so crucial to their success. And now not only did they know the size and shape their machine needed to be, but also had complete confidence they could build it and fly.

"The boys have finished their tables of the action of the wind on various surfaces, or rather they have finished their experiments," wrote Katharine to Milton, on December 7, 1901. "As soon as the results are put in tables, they will begin work for next season's bicycles."

Chapter Thirty Three

Getting back to business

The bicycle business in Dayton was seasonal, as it was in most cities north of the Mason-Dixon line. Spring and summer were the busy months for a bicycle shop. Folks didn't spend money on bicycles in the fall because they couldn't ride them in the winter. Bicycle shop owners like the Wrights spent the off-season catching up on repair work and building their spring stock.

In 1901 and 1902, the Wrights were building the mid-priced Van Cleve line of bicycles, started in 1896 and named after ancestors on their father's side of the family. In 1900, their catalog set the price for these custom-built bicycles between $32 and $47, depending on the "fittings" a buyer chose.

"The name Van Cleve has become the synonym of excellence in bicycle construction," read the catalog (presumably written by Wilbur).

In the same catalog, the Wrights announced the discontinuation of their St. Clair bicycle line, a cheaper product, to focus all their attention on the Van Cleve. But the brothers didn't abandon their budget customers. A 22- or 24-inch frame with name-brand fittings and good tires could be purchased for just $35. The price even included a bicycle wrench and tire pump. In the words of the catalog's author: "This is a genuine Van Cleve at a very low price."

If the Wrights published a catalog in 1901, all record of it has been lost. In all likelihood, they didn't. Their energies by this time were rolling in a whole new direction although no one, including the brothers themselves, seemed to fully realize the fact. Family correspondence and journals give no clue that anyone expected aeroplanes to become their life's work.

But throughout the winter, letters continued to flow between Wilbur and Chanute, the elder aviation engineer who considered the brothers his protégés.

"At least two thirds of my time in the past six months has been devoted to aeronautical matters," wrote Wilbur to Chanute on December 15. "Unless I decide to devote myself to something other than a business career I must give closer attention to my regular work for awhile."

A couple of weeks later, Wilbur wrote to Spratt: "We stopped experimenting about two weeks ago and shall probably not be able to resume them till next fall as our busy season is about here."

By the close of 1901, Chanute believed the Wrights were closer than anyone else to unlocking the secrets of flight. He encouraged Wilbur to set the bicycle business aside and devote his time to aeronautics. "I very much regret in the interest of science that you have reached a stopping place, for further experimenting on your part promises important results . . . If however some

Andrew Carnegie, American philanthropist
Lib. of Cong., Prints & Photos Div.
LC-DIG-pprs-3c01767t

rich man should give you $10,000 a year to go on, to connect his name with progress, would you do so? I happen to know Andrew Carnegie. Would you like for me to write to him?" asked Chanute in December.

"I do not think it would be wise for me to accept help . . . unless it was with the intention of cutting loose from business entirely and taking up a different line of lifework," replied Wilbur, belying his own ambivalence about the importance of his experiments. "There are limits to the neglect that business will endure, and a little pay for the time spent in neglecting it would only increase the neglect, without bringing in enough to offset the damage resulting from a wrecked business."

In spite of his intention to concentrate on bicycles, Wilbur couldn't resist writing a voluminous letter to Chanute in early January filled with charts and calculations from the brothers' wind tunnel data and Wilbur's theories on what the data meant. He was still working on the data and would send more later, he promised. The long letters filled with data con-

Katharine Wright (left) and a friend in the kitchen on Hawthorn Street
Lib. of Cong., Prints & Photos Div. LC-DIG-pprs-00533v

tinued into March, by which time Wilbur was thinking not only of building a glider for himself but undertaking the construction of a glider for Chanute as well. "We would doubtless have to commit the actual work to other hands but would give it our careful supervision," wrote Wilbur. As it turned out, Chanute decided to let Augustus Herring build his glider—a move that brought Herring into the Wrights' camp and set the stage for later aggravation. But at the time, the Wrights were relieved the work was going to someone else. "The building of machines for other men to risk their necks on is not a task that I particularly relish," Wilbur wrote to Chanute.

By late spring, work on plans for the 1902 glider had progressed far enough that Wilbur was anxious to leave for Kitty Hawk. But the previous year had taught him that summer was not the ideal time for flying experiments on the Outer Banks. Besides, Wilbur was helping his father with one of Milton's many lawsuits involving his role as a United Brethren in Christ bishop. Wilbur spent several days in Huntington, Indiana, site of the trial, in March, May and August.

In late August, Katharine wrote to Milton, "Will and Orv . . . are talking of going [to Kitty Hawk] next Monday, though sometimes Will thinks he would like to stay and see what happens at Huntington next week. They really ought to get away for awhile. Will is thin and nervous and so is Orv. . . . The flying machine is in process of making now. Will spins the sewing machine around by the hour while Orv squats around marking the places to sew."

1902

Looking south from Kitty Hawk village to Kill Devil Hill
Lib. of Cong., Prints & Photos Div. LC-DIG-pprs-00575v

Chapter Thirty Four

Returning to camp

Wilbur and Orville left Dayton for the Outer Banks at 9 a.m. on August 25. Once again they traveled by train to Elizabeth City, via Norfolk. Arriving in Elizabeth City late in the afternoon, August 26, they had already made arrangements to spend the night when they happened upon a Kitty Hawker at the docks, ready to sail for the Outer Banks.

Capt. Franklin Midgett offered the men passage on his freight boat, the *Lou Willis*. The Wrights scrambled around town, retrieving their baggage and picking up last minute provisions. The *Lou Willis* left for Kitty Hawk at 3:45 a.m. but a lack of wind kept them from making any progress. "By 3 o'clock we had made about 15 miles, about 1-1/3 miles an hour for eleven hours' sailing," wrote Wilbur to his father a couple days later. "As the captain saw there was no hope of getting to Kitty Hawk till long after midnight he decided to cast anchor till daylight next morning."

Midgett set sail at 4:30 a.m. and tied up at the Kitty Hawk docks nearly 12 hours later. It was a 36-hour boat trip, noted Orville in his diary, longer than the trip from Dayton to Elizabeth City.

Once at Kitty Hawk, the brothers rounded up Dan Tate with his spritsail boat and a horse-drawn cart to move their baggage to the Kill Devil Hill campsite. Dan, half-brother to Bill Tate, was the father of Tom Tate, the young boy who manned the Wrights' 1900 glider when full-grown men proved too heavy for the craft. Bill, the Wrights' genial host the previous two years, was busy with other work.

Long trip aside, there's no question the Wrights were pleased to be back. "They will be all right when they get down in the sand," wrote Katharine to their father shortly before they left Dayton. "They think life at Kitty Hawk cures all ills you know." In his own letter to Milton after reaching camp, Wilbur made their pleasure clear: "We got our stove to work and made some beef-extract soup, and this with crackers made us a little supper, and we went to bed happy."

The Wrights spent their first week back at camp working on their accommodations. The shed they built the previous year to house their glider was standing but in need of repairs. Having no experience with Outer Banks construction, they had set the building directly on the sand. "During the year the winds blew all the foundation, which consisted of sand, out from under the building and let the ends drop down two feet, thus giving the roof a shape like that of a dromedary's back," wrote Wilbur to Chanute shortly after arriving at camp. "We were a little discouraged at first but after two days' work we raised it to its original level and put foundation posts under it."

The Wrights' camp kitchen in 1902
(photo water damaged)
Lib. of Cong., Prints & Photos Div. LC-DIG-pprs-00575v

They brought lumber to enlarge the building, adding space for a kitchen and dining room, and a loft for sleeping. They worked on the kitchen first, according to Orville's journal, and took a picture of the area when it was all arranged. The photograph shows an impressively organized, well-stocked and efficient space, with special shelves for fresh eggs and a large produce bin. They spent time upholstering their dining chairs with excelsior-stuffed burlap "and have put in other royal luxuries," Wilbur wrote to Katharine.

The brothers also sunk a new well, 16 feet deep, giving them a reliable, potable water supply for the first time. And they assembled a bicycle, designed for riding in sand, that cut their three-hour trip to the village down to one.

"Everything is so much more favorable this year than last that it would be a pity to have your ideas of camp life here based on your experience of one year ago," wrote Wilbur to George Spratt, encouraging him to join them at Kitty Hawk. "First, we have not seen a dozen mosquitos in the two weeks and a half we have been here. Second, we fitted up our living arrangements much more comfortably than last year. Our kitchen is immensely improved, and then we have made beds on the second floor and now sleep aloft. It is an improvement over cots. We have put battens on the cracks of the whole building including the addition, so it is much tighter and waterproof than before as well as more sandproof. . . . No Huffaker and no mosquitoes, so we are having a splendid time."

The plague of mosquitoes suffered in 1901 was replaced by vermin, although the Wrights handled this new invasion with better humor—and more success. "At 11 o'clock last night I was awakened by the mouse crawling over my face. . . . " wrote Orville in his diary. "I found on getting up that the little fellow had only come to tell me to put another piece of cornbread in the trap. He had disposed of the first piece. I have sworn 'vengeance' on the little fellow for this impudence and insult." Several days later he noted, "The smart little mouse was found dead under trunk."

On September 8, after taking care of creature comforts and getting all their supplies and equipment in order, they began working on the new glider. As the new glider took shape, the brothers dismantled the 1901 glider that had been stored in the shed, using some of the pieces on the new machine. A week later this machine, like its predecessor, was history—captured in a few photographs, preserved in the Wrights' meticulous notes and drawings but lost as an artifact of flight.

Chapter Thirty Five

The 1902 glider

According to Tom Crouch, author of *The Bishop's Boys*, the 1902 glider was "radically different" in appearance than the Wrights' previous machines. The wing surface was 395 square feet, only 15 square feet larger than the 1901 machine, while the length of its wings was six times their width, rather than the 1:3 ratio used on the 1900 and 1901 gliders. The arch of the wing was smaller than 1901 and it peaked further back on the wing surface. "The span was over 10 feet longer than in 1901 and the chord two feet shorter. To a modern eye, the 1900 and 1901 gliders seem bulky and cumbersome, with their stubby rectangular wings. The 1902 craft, lighter and more graceful, looks like an airplane."

The 1901 machine's bulky rectangular front elevator was replaced by "a trim ellipsoid rudder," said Fred Howard in *Wilbur and Orville*.

Although wing-warping was the Wrights' innovative solution for controlling their flying machines, their method of achieving this control had its problems. As Crouch explained it, wing-warping increased lift but also created drag resulting in a kind of skidding motion. In 1902, the Wrights added a "two-surface fixed vertical rudder at the rear" designed to counteract some of the drag and inherent control problems caused by wing-warping. According to Howard, the ever-practical Wrights had attached the new rudder with hinged spars so that the tail would swing upward if it struck the ground when landing.

The Wrights' first gliders had wing-warping mechanisms worked by the operator's feet. Some biographers have written that the switch to a hip-operated cradle took place during the 1901 flying season; others place the change in 1902. "Although it kept the operator from slipping sidewise down the wing in a turn," wrote Howard, explaining the switch (which he placed in 1902). "It was hard on the hipbones, which, in the case of the Wright brothers, had little natural padding. Eventually, they padded the cradle for greater comfort."

Like the 1901 machine, the 1902 glider was covered with Pride of the

West muslin. They improved its application with stronger ties and varnish. Skids were added to the underside of the machine to keep it from digging into the sand when landing.

They began flying the new glider on September 19 and were delighted to find that it glided on an angle of seven degrees or less. At the end of the day, Orville wrote in his diary that "we are convinced that the trouble with the 1901 machine is overcome by the vertical tail."

By the time the Wrights left Kitty Hawk on October 24, they had made close to 1,000 glides, increasing their distance to 622.5 feet and staying in the air as long as 26 seconds without a serious mishap. Those numbers, as impressive as they were for that time, don't tell the full story of what they achieved that summer. Their real success lay in the design changes to their glider that were yet to come.

Chapter Thirty Six

The missing piece

The Wrights planned to stay at Kitty Hawk about two months. They expected Chanute to show up for a week or two with Augustus Herring to conduct tests on two gliders Chanute had shipped to their camp. In exchange for their room and board, such as it was, the two men would help the Wrights with their experiments. The Wrights had also invited George Spratt to return. They had found the doctor-turned-aviation engineer to be pleasant company and a good worker. His ability to discuss and understand aeronautics added greatly to his appeal. When Spratt begged off, Wilbur wrote him the long letter quoted in Chapter 34, and convinced him to make the trip.

But no one could come to Kitty Hawk before October, so the Wrights spent the first month working on their own with the help of Dan Tate. Dan had helped the Wrights intermittently in the previous years and worked for them throughout their 1902 stay and for part of the fall in 1903, although their working relationship was not the best. Dan marched to his own tune. Working hours were dictated by his main occupation, commercial fishing. He was influenced by a run of bluefish, the weather, or the needs of family and friends. It was a work ethic the Wrights didn't understand.

But Dan was present September 23 when the glider with Orville at the controls reared up and stalled. "The result was a heap of flying machine, cloth, and sticks . . . with me in the center without a bruise or a scratch," noted Orville in his diary that night. "In spite of this sad catas-

Dan Tate helping Wilbur fly 1902 glider
Lib. of Cong., Prints & Photos Div. LC-DIG-pprs-00631v

trophe we are tonight in a hilarious mood as a a result of the encouraging performance of the machine both in control and in angles of flight."

Orville's stall was the second in less than a week. The first occurred with Wilbur at the controls on September 20. Both incidents were compounded by their unfamiliarity with changes they made to the rudder controls on September 19. When Wilbur described his experience, he said that his confusion about which way to move the rudder control caused the machine to instantly rear up "as though bent on a mad attempt to pierce the heavens. But after a moment it seemed to perceive the folly of such an undertaking and gradually slowed up till it came almost to a stop with the front of the machine still pointing heavenward. . . ." Wilbur was able to reverse the rudder and "by the time the ground was reached it was under fair control."

As a result of Wilbur's stall, they adjusted the wings which had been assembled with the spars "straight from tip to tip," said Orville in *How We Invented the Airplane*." They arched the surfaces, making the tips "at least four inches lower than the center. We also made the angle of the surfaces at the tips greater than the angle at the center of the machine." While these changes helped, they didn't help enough as evidenced by Orville's mishap two days later.

Serious stalling—something the Wrights referred to as "well digging"—had not presented itself before 1902 because their original tailless glider featured a front elevator which "was extremely effective in reducing the violent reaction of a stall," explained Peter Jakab in *Visions of a Flying Machine*. Although the Wrights didn't know it at the time, the fixed-wing design they favored—as did most airplane builders after them—was inherently prone to stalls. Elements of the 1902 glider's new design (particularly the tail) that allowed it to soar higher and stay in the air longer made it more prone to stall. It was a problem they needed to solve.

Lorin Wright arrived at camp for a two-week stay on September 30, followed the next day by Spratt, who stayed until October 20. Shortly after their arrival, Orville—who some biographers claim was suffering insomnia from drinking too much coffee during their nightly gab

fest—came up with the final solution to gaining full control of their glider. "While lying awake last night," wrote Orville in his diary (without
mentioning the coffee), "I studied out a new vertical rudder."

Orville suggested a new moveable rudder to replace the fixed tail
vane at breakfast the next morning. After thinking about it for a moment,
Wilbur suggested interconnecting the rudder to the wing-warping mechanism. By that afternoon,"we began making new vertical rudder, one that
is operated at same time as end tips," Orville wrote in his diary. "We made
it with only one surface 5 feet by 14 inches, which we think will be suf-
ficient."

According to Orville 's account in *How We Invented the Airplane*, the
brothers had already tried removing one vane of the tail rudder shortly
after one of the stalls but found that it made little difference. This adjustment isn't referred to in their daily logs but it could very well have been
done when they reassembled the glider after Orville's mishap.

The day after making the rudder change, Chanute and Herring arrived
at camp for a nine-day stay. Rain, conversation, rearranging the camp to
accommodate extra bodies and assembling Chanute's gliders kept the
Wrights from putting their
revised machine back in the air
until the 8th of October.
Although they flew it a few times
while Chanute and Herring were
in camp, it seems they avoided
working on their own experiments—probably to avoid
revealing too much to Herring.
(Their caution was justified.
After their success in 1903,
Herring tried to bully them into a

Wilbur gliding on Oct. 24, 1902, with the
single rear rudder clearly visible
Lib. of Cong., Prints & Photos Div. LC-DIG-pprs-00601v

partnership by claiming credit for part of their work, based on his brief
visit.) They spent most of the next week helping test Chanute's two
machines, both of which turned out to be complete failures. It wasn't
until after Lorin, then Chanute and Herring, left Kitty Hawk that the

brothers finally got back in the air.

"Wilbur covered more than 300 feet on several glides, but far more significant, was the fact that now he was maneuvering the glider through the same motions that had almost killed Orville and him before—and was doing so with complete control and balance throughout." wrote Harry Combs in *Kill Devil Hill.* "Where entry into a steep bank condition before meant loss of control and a frightening swerve into the deadly spin, Wilbur was able to glide almost straight out. . . . Out of this situation, which had killed everyone who had ever entered it, he would nose down and turn . . . making perfectly controlled descents. . . . They were over-joyed with their performance."

"The past five days have been the most satisfactory for gliding that we have had," wrote Orville to Katharine on October 23. "In two days we made over 250 glides, or more than we had made all together up to the time Lorin left. We have gained considerable proficiency in the handling of the machine now, so that we are able to take it out in any kind of weath-er."

The new moveable tail rudder and its attachment to the wing-warp-ing mechanism was the final piece to the Wrights' solution for controlling an aircraft. This idea and its implementation, wrote Howard, "were to have even more important consequences than those that followed Wilbur's twisting of an empty inner tube box. . . . What the Wrights had stumbled on . . . was the discovery that the principal function of the ver-tical rudder in an aircraft is not to steer but to supplement and refine the action of the lateral control mechanism. This was not an insignificant dis-covery, for it completed and brought to a patentable stage the Wrights' three-dimensional system of airplane control, which is the basic system used today in all winged vehicles that depend on the atmosphere for their support."

(Howard may have overstated his case here. There were those who would argue later, in the course of the Wrights' patent wars, that while the basic principles the Wrights developed and proved were correct, their "system," as such, was not the best means of achieving the control they described. Others followed on the heels of the Wrights and invented better ways to achieve control.)

October 24 marked the end of the Wrights' gliding this season. They spent the next three days closing up the camp and packing their glider—and the two machines left behind by Chanute—into the shed. Then they walked the 4 miles to Kitty Hawk village, probably spending the night at Capt. Franklin Midgett's house.

"We left Kitty Hawk at daybreak [on October 28] . . . after a very exciting but tiresome trip," wrote Wilbur to Chanute. "Into the last ten days of practice we crowded more glides than in all the weeks preceding. . . . This practice enabled us to greatly increase our skill in the management of the machine. . . . We should have liked to have prolonged our stay a few weeks longer but Mr. [William] Tate had engaged himself to take charge of a fishing crew and the men wished to open the season Oct. 27th so we decided to return before our tickets expired."

Orville making right turn, showing warping of wings on October 24, 1902
Lib. of Cong., Prints & Photos Div. LC-DIG-pprs-00599v

This year, when the Wrights headed back to Dayton, they were certain they would return to the Outer Banks. Already they were making plans for the year that would change aviation history. Nearly a month earlier, Wilbur had written to his father, hinting at where the brothers were headed. "We have far beaten all records for flatness of glides. . . . This means that in soaring we can descend much slower, and in a power machine can fly with much less power. . . . Everything is so much more satisfactory that we now believe that the flying problem is really nearing its solution."

"The fore-and-aft control of the 1902 machine had proved very effective," wrote Orville some years later. "So that when at last we felt that the problem of lateral equilibrium had been entirely solved, we began to turn our thoughts to the construction of a machine to be driven with a motor."

In early December, the Wrights wrote to at least 10 companies inquiring about gasoline engines which would "develop 8 to 9 brake H.P., would weigh no more than 180 lbs. or an average of 20 lbs. per H.P., and would be free from vibration." None could meet their specifications.

1903

The first successful powered, heavier-than-air flight with Orville at the controls
Lib. of Cong., Prints & Photos Div. LC-DIG-pprs-00626v

Chapter Thirty Seven

Push and pull

By the time Wilbur and Orville left Kitty Hawk in late 1902, they had logged over 1,000 glides in three years, although their total time in the air was under four hours. Only Lilienthal had spent more time aloft (although it had taken him five years to do it). And, the Wrights had solved most of the problems of stability and control in flight. Some aviation historians have suggested that, at that point, their legacy of invention was essentially complete.

In its final form, the "1902 glider was the first fully controllable aircraft," wrote Peter Jakab in *Visions of a Flying Machine*. " It was the realization of the Wrights' conceptual understanding that an aircraft operates in three dimensions and cannot rely solely on inherent stability for successful flight. Every airplane following the Wrights' has used three-axis control to fly. It was the core claim of their later flying machine

Front view of the 1903 Wright Flyer
Lib. of Cong., Prints & Photos Div. LC-DIG-pprs-00615v

patent and the principal reason the powered airplane that lifted off the beach at Kitty Hawk in December 1903 is regarded as the world's first."

But the Wrights had one more significant contribution to make to aeronautical science.

Heading into 1903, they assumed that adding power to the glider would be one of their easier accomplishments. Gasoline engine technology was making great strides due to the growing demand for automobiles. If outside sources failed, they had already built their own small gas-powered engine to drive tools in their shop and they were certain they could build another.

As for propellers, they expected to draw on existing marine screw technology. Several well-known engineers—Chanute and Langley among them—believed that pushing or pulling an airplane through air was no different than propelling a ship through water. The brothers, who hadn't really studied the problem until now, assumed these educated men to be correct.

By early 1903, the Wrights were immersed in propulsion. "What at first seemed a simple problem became more complex the longer we studied it," wrote Orville in *Century* magazine in 1908. "With the machine moving forward, the air flying backward, the propellers turning sidewise, and nothing standing still, it seemed impossible to find a starting point from which to trace the various simultaneous reactions. Contemplation of it was confusing."

"I think the hardest job Will and Orv had was with the propellers," said Charlie Taylor, their mechanic, in an interview published in *Colliers Weekly* in 1948. "I don't believe they ever were given enough credit for that development, They had read up on all that was published about boat propellers, but they couldn't find any formula for what they needed, So they had to develop their own. . . . They concluded that an air propeller was really just a rotating wing, and by experimenting in the wind box they arrived at the design they wanted."

While other aviation experimenters had thought about using propellers, and some had actually attached them to a variety of flying machines, none had been "willing to invest time and energy in studies of propeller efficiency," explained Crouch in *Heirs to Prometheus*. "The inadequate conception of the 'air screw' boring through air was retained until overthrown by the brilliant Wright treatment of the propeller as a rotary wing."

"We worked out a theory of our own on the subject, and soon discovered, as we usually do, that all the propellers built heretofore are all wrong, and then built a pair of propellers . . . based on our theory, which are all right!" Orville wrote to George Spratt in June 1903.

Drawing on their previous wind tunnel work and new experiments carried out to test their newly developed theories of air propulsion, the Wrights designed a propeller that both worked for them and worked as much as 20 percent more efficiently than propellers built for marine use. They "laid another key building block on the foundation of aeronautical engineering," wrote Jakab. "This conceptual work was a breakthrough comparable to wing-warping, requiring creativity "as imaginative as the design of the wind tunnel balances."

Once the Wrights understood the theory behind an efficient rotary wing and had test data to support it, they built two propellers out of glued wood, hand-shaped with a hatchet and drawshave. They worried that mounting the turning blades in front of the wings would disrupt air flow, affecting the performance of the plane. So when the machine was finally assembled, they mounted the propellers behind the wings. They also designed the propellers to turn in opposite directions, so that any effect on the lateral movement of the plane was equalized.

Chapter Thirty Eight

Power to fly

"Unlike their predecessors, who had focused on the propulsion problem separately, the Wrights considered power requirements in terms of the aerodynamic qualities of the aircraft," explained Jakab. The propellers, engine and the flying machine itself were all interdependent, and progress on their design and manufacture proceeded somewhat simultaneously.

When no supplier could be found to provide a gasoline motor meeting their specifications, the Wrights built their own. Working with their mechanic, Charlie Taylor, they spent six weeks building a 4 cylinder, water-cooled engine they hoped would generate enough horsepower to achieve a minimum air speed of 23 mph. The four in-line horizontal cylinders were made of cast iron, while the crankcase was a single piece of cast aluminum alloy. The crankshaft was high carbon tool steel. There was no water pump. A slim radiator made from flattened metal tubing provided minimal cooling, allowing the engine to run for only a few minutes before it overheated. There was no fuel pump. Gasoline was gravity-fed from a 1.5- quart tank suspended above the engine. There was also no carburetor. The cylinders were primed with a few drops of gasoline and ignited with a spark from four dry-cell batteries which weren't carried on the plane. Once the engine started, a switch was thrown, starting a low-tension magneto driven by a 27-pound flywheel to supply current while the engine was running. The speed of the engine could be adjusted only by changing the timing of the spark, something that was practical to do only while the plane was on the ground.

The engine had enough gasoline to last 18 minutes and might have carried the plane as far as 10 miles, depending on the wind, said Harry Combs in *Kill Devil Hill*. Whether it could have withstood its own heat is another matter.

The engine was crude but certainly not as primitive as it sounds today. With the exception of what it lacked—a fuel pump, water pump and carburetor, all left off as much out of concern for the weight of the engine as anything else—it was the equivalent of the automobile engine of their day.

The Wrights had determined that 8 hp were necessary to power their airplane and had hoped the engine would weigh less than 180 pounds. When completely assembled with fuel and water, the engine weighed close to the target, but its performance was better than anticipated, producing about 12 hp. They were pleased with the performance of their makeshift motor, said biographer Fred Kelly in *The Wright Brothers.* "Long afterward they found out that the engine should have provided about twice as much power as it did. The trouble, as they later said, was their 'lack of experience in building gasoline motors.'"

The engine powered the propellers through a system of sprockets and chains, similar to the way power was transmitted from pedals to the wheels of a bicycle. To make the propellers spin in opposite directions, they crossed the chains in a simple figure eight. To keep them from flapping in the wind, the chains were run inside metal tubes. It was all ingeniously simple and, no doubt, another instance where their experience with bicycles served them well.

1903 engine in the Wrights' shop in Dayton
Lib. of Cong., Prints & Photos Div. LC-DIG-pprs-00627v

Chapter Thirty Nine

The first Flyer

The airplane itself was not radically different from the 1902 glider. The wingspan was just over 40 feet with a camber (arch) of 1:20, slightly flatter than their 1902 design, with six feet between the wings. The total wing area was 510 square feet.

One of the more subtle changes was the plane's asymmetrical design.

The engine sat to the right of center on the bottom wing, according to Combs. The pilot, who weighed less than the engine, was off-center to the left. To provide enough lift for the extra weight, the right wings were a few inches longer than the left.

The ribs of their glider wings had been built from solid, steam-bent wood. For the Flyer, these horizontal supports were built from two thin strips of ash separated by blocks and reinforced at the joints with glued paper. The wings were then covered top and bottom with Pride of the West muslin, cut and sewn on the bias for added stiffness. The gliders had fabric only on the top side of each wing. Once again the Wrights trussed the wings to droop, so that the wing tips were nearly a foot lower than the center on both sides to reduce the effect of crosswinds.

The 1903 glider, in Dayton, before it was dismantled and shipped to Kitty Hawk where the engine was added
Photo courtesy Outer Banks History Center

They also changed the shape of the wood struts which separated and supported the wings vertically. Up until this time, it had always been assumed that a teardrop shape—presenting a rounded edge to the wind and tapering to the back—was the most aerodynamic. But their wind tunnel tests showed that a rectangular form with all corners slightly rounded was significantly better. This was a finding that Chanute, a well-educated engineer, found difficult to believe, but the Wrights used their findings anyway. They were, of course, right.

Additional stabilization for the wing was gained by running thin, multi-strand wire the length of the wing through the uprights. It was the same wire John Roebling used to build the Brooklyn Bridge, according to Fred Howard in *Wilbur and Orville*. It was "an incredibly clever, yet simple, means of adequately supporting the wing surfaces without using excessively broad, and therefore heavy, struts," said Jakab. Stay wires were also added between the front and rear uprights to make all but the wing tips stationary. "Only the rear outer edges of both wings could now be flexed, much like the movement of ailerons on a modern aircraft," explained Howard.

The Wright brothers went back to twin rear rudders and increased the surface area of the rudders to more than 20 square feet. The double rudder was something they had tried on the 1902 glider in a fixed position but later changed. They kept the moveable rudder linked to the wing-warping system, a change made on the 1902 glider and refined in gliding experiments this year before the Flyer was assembled. These controls were attached to the hip cradle in which the pilot lay on the lower wing. The front elevators, with a combined surface of 58 square feet, were given an elliptical shape and a "more substantial spruce framework," said Jakab. As in the 1902 glider, they moved in tandem with a single hand lever.

Two parallel skids under the machine were redesigned and braced, said Howard "to withstand the impact of landing the much heavier Flyer which was now 21 feet long and, without the pilot or fuel on board, weighed over 600 pounds. The 1902 glider barely weighed 100.

Chapter Forty

Time to fly

When the summer of 1903 rolled around, Wilbur and Orville were anxious to get back to Kitty Hawk. But, as Howard pointed out, "Each trip to the Outer Banks had seen a staggering increase in the amount of goods and supplies needed to see them through the season. . . . In 1903 they had to transport not only a flying machine . . . but an imposing collection of tools and equipment. Their array of instruments included their new French anemometer, their clinometer, binoculars for birdwatching, camera and tripod and a supply of glass-plate negatives, stopwatches, tachometers, and a coil box with batteries for starting their motor. There

Elizabeth City docks near the turn of the century
Photo courtesy Museum of the Albemarle

were rifles for sport and game, plenty of bedding for late-autumn nights, burlap for making new patent beds among the rafters, mosquito netting, reading materials, French and German grammars, even a worn carpet or two to hang against the windy walls of their drafty living room."

It was September 23 before the Wrights left Dayton, after shipping the plane and most of their supplies separately. For the first time, they went from Elizabeth City to Manteo and hired a boat there to take them to Kitty Hawk. And also for the first time they made the entire trip in just over two days, arriving at their camp on the afternoon of the 25th.

The men spent the next two weeks repairing the old camp building, which had been knocked off its foundation during a winter storm, and building a new shed to house the Flyer. Just a few feet from the old shed that housed the 1902 glider and served as the camp's living quarters, this new building was larger and featured hinged "garage" doors at each end. Dan Tate was hired to help with the work.

Wilbur and Orville assembling the 1903 machine at Kitty Hawk
Lib. of Cong., Prints & Photos Div. LC-DIG-pprs-00656v

The Flyer didn't arrive until October 8 so when weather conditions allowed, they practiced gliding with the 1902 machine and made a few minor modifications to the glider's rear rudder, enlarging its surface area and the way it was attached to its frame. They began assembling the Flyer the day after it arrived, but they had no intentions of flying it before they completed experiments with the glider. "It will probably be nearly Nov. 1st before we are ready for trial, especially if we have some nice soaring weather," wrote Wilbur to Chanute on October 16.

The next few days did bring good soaring weather and the brothers made progress with their gliding experiments. George Spratt, invited by the Wrights to witness their attempt at powered flight, arrived at camp on October 23. Three days later, Orville set a gliding record of 1 minute, 11.8 seconds, that stood until he broke it himself eight years later.

By the next week, assembly of the Flyer was running behind schedule and the weather had turned miserably cold. According to Orville's diary, they had trouble installing the trussing wires "which for some reason unexplainable failed to fit." A few days later, Orville reported that the propeller shafts, made from tubular steel, were vibrating so much that the propellers couldn't be tightened properly. One of them twisted out of alignment. The shafts needed work. The magneto wasn't producing an adequate spark, either. He estimated it would take at least 10 days to solve the problems.

With no flying in the near future and suffering from the cold, Spratt decided to head home. He shipped the propeller shafts to Charlie Taylor in Dayton for repairs on his way through Manteo. While in Manteo, he met Chanute, who was just arriving on the Outer Banks, hoping to witness the first flights. Spratt was not optimistic in his assessment of the state of things at the Kill Devil Hill camp. After the Wrights' finally got their Flyer off the ground, Chanute chided Spratt, "You now know that you were in error in your apprehensions of disaster. . . ."

This visit in 1903 marked the last time Spratt would work with the Wrights although they remained on friendly terms for several more years. Spratt continued to experiment with airplane design, preferring a pivot-wing design because it offered the possibility for "automatic" control. His earlier association with Chanute grew out of the idea that a plane should have inherent stability and thus no need for pilot control. It was an idea the Wrights did not share. According to Marvin McFarland in *Heirs to Prometheus*, "The Wrights conceived of the airplane as an essentially unstable vehicle that had to be managed in the air." Largely because their lead was followed, most airplanes built in the 20th century were built under this assumption. They could have been built differently.

Chanute stayed at the Kill Devil Hill camp six days. Only a couple days were suitable for gliding; most were still bitterly cold. The men spent much of the time talking about flying and their plans for the coming year. After Chanute left, Wilbur and Orville were alone for the first time in nearly a month. They tested various parts of the Flyer and experimented with their instruments while waiting for the repaired propeller shafts to arrive. Gliding experiments were out because the wood frame of the year-old glider had become dangerously dry due to the heat stove fire they kept burning in the shed to keep themselves warm. "It is so rickety as to be unsafe for gliding in high winds," wrote Orville to his sister on November 15. "We have now probably made our last glides on it."

The repaired shafts arrived back at camp on November 20 and the Wrights immediately installed them and tried to test the propulsion system. The magneto was still not functioning properly, and the sprockets connecting the drive chains to the propellers wouldn't stay tight. The next day, in desperation, they locked the sprockets on with tire cement. Over the next week, they completed the launching mechanism they had begun building when Spratt was at camp.

The Wrights' choice of a rail for launching and skids for landing made sense for the sands at Kitty Hawk. For some undisclosed reason —although weight concerns might have been a factor—they continued to use these methods (later adding a weighted derrick to give the plane an initial push) long after Glenn Curtiss and other airplane builders had proved wheels were a more practical choice for most other locations.

In any case, in 1903 the Flyer was launched off a 60-foot monorail made of four 2x4's. The top side of the boards was covered with a thin metal strip. Rather than riding directly on the rail, the skids of the machine rested on a 6-foot plank which, in turn, was supported by a small

1903 machine on the launching track at Big Kill Devil Hill
Lib. of Cong., Prints & Photos Div. LC-DIG-pprs-00612v

wooden truck on two metal ball-bearing rollers, one in front of the other, made from modified bicycle hubs. A third bicycle hub supported the front rudder to keep the machine upright on the track.

"Our track for starting the machine (total cost about $4.00) amused Mr. Chanute considerably, as Langley is said to have spent nearly $50,000.00 on his starting device which failed in the end to give a proper start," wrote Wilbur to his father.

On November 28, a propeller shaft cracked during tests. The Wrights decided Orville would return to Dayton and make a new pair out of solid spring steel. Time was running out. They had promised the family they'd be home by Christmas and winter weather was setting in. Although Outer Banks winters were far milder than what they were accustomed to in Ohio, they did not have adequate shelter or clothing to live and work in the freezing temperatures whipped even lower by high winds. And their supplies of food and other goods brought from home were nearly gone.

Orville returned to camp on December 11 and the brothers abandoned their plans for more ground tests of the Flyer, deciding to fly as soon as possible. They needed help to launch the glider and realized that if they were successful, they would need witnesses to confirm what they'd done. Dan Tate had walked off the job in a dispute of gathering firewood in late October and hadn't been back since. Bill Tate had moved from the village to Martin's Point and was too far away to summon on short notice. So they arranged for men from the Kill Devil Hills Life-Saving Station to come help whenever they tacked a large red flag to the side of their shed.

December 14 was the first suitable day although the wind, at 5 mph, was lighter than they wanted. Bob Westcott, John T. Daniels, Tom Beacham, W. S. Dough and Ben O'Neal came from the lifesaving station and helped the Wrights move the machine from the shed to the big hill. They laid the launching rail on the incline, hoping to give the plane some extra momentum for lift-off to compensate for the lack of wind. Wilbur won a coin toss to make the first try. The track was not laid straight down the hill nor was it pointed directly into the wind making his take-off shaky, at best. He immediately learned that the newly designed front elevator was extremely sensitive. After just 3.5 seconds in the air, he stalled the machine 15 feet in the air, started to recover, but struck the ground about 100 feet downhill from where he went airborne. The landing did minor damage to the machine, putting an end to flying until it could be repaired.

"The machinery all worked in entirely satisfactory manner, and seems reliable," Wilbur wrote that evening to his sister and father. "The power is ample, and but for a trifling error due to lack of experience with this machine and this method of starting the machine would undoubtedly have flown beautifully."

Even though the plane got off the ground and traveled some distance, it did not meet the Wrights' criteria for successful powered flight. Time in the air and distance traveled, though short, were not the issues. Rather, the flight was disqualified in their minds because the plane, taking off down a hill, landed at a lower point, raising the question of whether or not it had traveled under its own power or simply moved with the forces of gravity. The other key issue, especially for the Wrights, was whether the flight proved the pilot had control of the machine. In this case, it appeared the answer was no. But the flight was enough to prove to themselves, without question, that they could—and would—fly. "Success assured," Wilbur told his father in a telegram sent the next day.

December 15 was spent making repairs to the Flyer. Repairs were finished on the 16th, but the wind wasn't strong enough to fly. When the brothers woke up on December 17, the wind was blowing 20 to 25 mph. This time, their signal for help brought three crewmen from the lifesaving station—John T. Daniels, W. S. Dough, and A. D. Etheridge—and W. C. Brinkley, a lumber buyer from Manteo who happened to be at the station on business, and Johnny Moore, a teenager from Nags Head who may have been visiting at the station (or may have just happened to come by at the right time—historians have been unable to say for sure).

Because Wilbur flew on the 14th, Orville was the first to pilot the Flyer on the 17th. This time the track was laid on flat ground closer to their camp. Orville set up his camera and asked John Daniels to squeeze the shutter release as soon as the plane took off. The photo, now famous, came out beautifully. Wright biographer Howard explained: The Flyer reached an air speed of nearly 30 mph as it lifted off the rail but because it was traveling into a 20 mph wind, the ground speed was around 7 mph as Daniels snapped the photo, "making it possible to record the start of the flight on one of the slow photographic plates of 1903, even though the sky was overcast."

Orville travelled an estimated 120 feet at an average altitude of 8 to 10 feet in 12 seconds in his first flight. He also had trouble with the touchy front elevator and flew

Orville piloting the third flight on
December 17, 1903
Lib. of Cong., Prints & Photos Div. LC-DIG-pprs-00628v

erratically. His landing, like Wilbur's on the 14th, was not planned and resulted in minor damage repaired in less than an hour. It could be argued that this flight fell short of controlled powered flight too—but, in light of the following three flights that ended with Wilbur covering 852 feet in 59 seconds, histo-

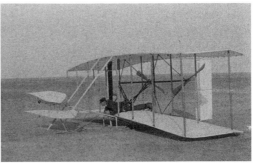

Wilbur landing after one of his two successful flights on December 17, 1903

Lib. of Cong., Prints & Photos Div. LC-DIG-pprs-00611r

rians have agreed that the first flight on the 17th adequately proved that the Wrights had reached their goal. In fact, none of the flights were smooth and none ended by pilot choice. Even so, they were the first in history to accomplish as much as they did. As Orville put it later, his flight was "the first in the history of the world in which a machine carrying a man had raised itself by its own power into the air in full flight, had sailed forward without reduction of speed, and had finally landed at a point as high as that from which it started."

In addition to Orville's initial short flight and Wilbur's final long one, Wilbur flew 175 feet in 12 seconds and Orville added 3 seconds to his time and flew 200 feet. They each achieved an altitude between 12 and 14 feet in these later flights. The machine was damaged again in landing after Wilbur's second flight. After being carried back to camp for repairs, the machine was picked up by a gust of wind, tumbled across the sand and wrecked. Wilbur and Orville had grabbed for the plane but were not strong enough to hold on. John T. Daniels, a large surfman, got hold of the machine and got tangled up inside the wing in the rigging wires. "Mr. Daniels, having had no experience in handling a machine of this kind, hung on to it from the inside, and as a result was knocked down and turned over and over with it as it went. His escape was miraculous, as he was in with the engine and chains," wrote Orville. Not only did Daniels get the distinction of witnessing and photographing the first flight, he became the Flyer's first casualty although his injuries were not serious.

With the machine wrecked, the Wrights began packing. The disintegrating 1902 glider was left behind as all their gliders had been but the 1903 Flyer was crated and shipped to Dayton. They left the Outer Banks on December 21.

Chapter Forty One

Getting out the news

On the afternoon of December 17, 1903, the Wrights walked to the Weather Bureau at the Kitty Hawk Life-Saving Station and asked Joe Dosher to send a telegram to their father: "Success four flights Thursday morning all against twenty-one mile wind started from level with engine power along average speed through air thirty-one miles longest 57 seconds inform press home Christmas." (The telegram misstated the time of the longest flight—it was 59 seconds).

The brothers had already made arrangements with their family to announce their success. Katharine was to send a telegram to Octave Chanute; Lorin was to write a short press release for the Dayton newspapers and Milton would field calls at home. While there's no question they wanted their achievement acknowledged, it's also clear that they had no intention of providing the kind of information most journalists want—and need—to cover a story of this magnitude. In 1903, in some people's minds, the idea that man could fly was the equivalent of sighting alien space ships today. For others, flight was a possibility but it was one tainted by so many crazy, false claims that proof was needed to be believed. In almost every case, the terse announcement prepared by Lorin for the press was simply not adequate and most of the Dayton newspapers—and the Associated Press in Dayton—refused to use the story.

The *Virginian-Pilot* in Norfolk, Va., was tipped off about the Wrights' flights on the afternoon of the 17th by the local telegraph operator who received Dosher's telegram to Milton. He didn't release the wording of the message but possibly encouraged by the words "inform press," told reporter Edward Dean that someone had flown an airplane on the Outer Banks. Dean took the news to his editor, Keville Glennan, who had sources in the lifesaving service and asked them to check the news and get details about the Wrights and the flights. In the meantime, another *Virginian-Pilot* employee, Harry Moore, heard the news from a different source. Moore never said who his source was, but it has been speculated that he had friends at one of the Outer Banks lifesaving stations. Due to the inaccuracy of his information, it is unlikely he spoke directly with any of the eyewitnesses to the flights. Glennan, faced with a confirmed story that he deemed newsworthy but few verified facts, decided to trust the accuracy of Moore's information and run with the scoop.

Wright biographers have been critical of the *Pilot*, in spite of their attempt to give the story serious coverage, and charged that Glennan and Moore made things up. Unable to get information directly from the Wrights, it's more likely they collected information from whomever they could find willing to talk on the Outer Banks, and much of that information was second-and third-hand. Even if reporters spoke directly to witnesses of the flight, none of these men had any experience with flying machines. Most had no concept of what manned, powered flight entailed and all were unqualified to describe it.

On the morning of December 18, the *Virginian-Pilot* ran the following banner headline on its front page: "Flying machine soars 3 miles in teeth of high wind over sand hills and waves at Kitty Hawk on Carolina Coast." Underneath were four smaller headlines: "No balloon attached to aid it; Two years of Hard, Secret Work by Two Ohio Brothers Crowned with Success; Accomplished what Langley Failed; and With Man as Passenger Huge Machine Flew Like Bird Under Perfect Control." The story went on to describe a machine that had one propeller mounted at the front and one mounted underneath. A "navigator's car" was suspended under the engine with a "huge fan-shaped rudder of canvas." The machine was launched down the side of a sand hill. With Wilbur Wright at the controls, not only did the flight cover 3 miles but it reached an altitude of 60 feet. According to the story, Wilbur jumped from the plane at flight's end and yelled "Eureka!"

The *Pilot* also reported that "Very little can be learned here about the Wrights. They are supposed by the natives of Kitty Hawk to be people of means and are always well dressed." The comment was typical of how "the natives" recalled the Wrights. Its inclusion lends credence to the probability that locals did contribute to the story in some way.

The *Virginian-Pilot's* story went out over the Associated Press wire from Norfolk, as did a separate story written by Harry Moore, and was picked up by a few newspapers around the country, most notably the *Washington Post* and *Chicago Record-Herald*. Undoubtedly due to the regional tie-in, the *Indianapolis Journal* and *Cincinnati Post* also followed up on the story, calling Milton Wright for photos and interviews. For the most part, it was viewed as too fantastic (which, indeed, it was) to be believed. Later, when accurate information about the Wrights and their accomplishment became available, "facts" from that first news report were still called up and repeated.

The Wrights evidently never considered the possibility that a newspaper near the Outer Banks might get wind of their flight and attempt to cover the event. Considering that the news was known at the Kitty Hawk and Kill Devil Hills Life-Saving Stations (both equipped with telephone service) and that it was sent to Dayton via telegram which required several men to read the message and re-key it as it made its way across the country, their belief that they could control the news was naive.

"Katharine got a telegram from Orville, saying he and Wilbur would be at home to night (sic). They came at 8:00," wrote Milton Wright in his diary on December 23. "They had some interviewers in the way, but supressed them." Katharine's telegram actually said, "Have survived perilous trip reported in papers. Home tonight," making it clear that Orville was well-aware of what had, so far, been published. However, the brothers refused to be interviewed at the train station, missing an opportunity to set the record straight before too much damage had been done. They waited until January 5, 1904, to issue a statement to the Associated Press, giving brief details of what happened on December 17.

Several biographers have also repeated the Wrights' claim that the press was not interested in their news. In fact, there was plenty of interest. According to Thomas Parramore in *Triumph at Kitty Hawk*, the Wrights received a telegram on December 18 from the *New York World* asking for exclusive rights to a story with pictures. Several more telegrams arrived from magazines, including *Woman's Home Companion*, *Scientific American ,*and *Century*. The Wrights gave two short interviews to the *Chicago Tribune* and the *New York World* on December 26 but were not very forthcoming with details. "We are giving no pictures nor descriptions of machine or methods at present," Wilbur wrote to Chanute two days later.

From this point on, given their penchant for mistrust and secrecy, their relationship with the press was an uncomfortable one.

The Long Road to Reward

Exterior view of the Wright Co. factory, Dayton, Ohio, 1911
Lib. of Cong., Prints & Photos Div. LC-DIG-pprs-00712v

Chapter Forty Two

Building a practical flying machine

The Wrights' invention of the airplane began as an informal scientific investigation by two men who enjoyed engineering challenges. Before television became America's number one pastime, tinkering was a popular hobby. Nearly every home had its workshop. Wilbur and Orville grew up in an age of invention: Electric lighting, indoor plumbing, gasoline engines and automobiles, radios, telephones and other conveniences we take for granted today were changing society at every turn. In the midst of such marvels, common men dreamed big dreams. Pursuits of such lofty ambitions were not uncommon in their time—only their success made them extraordinary.

"We had taken up aeronautics merely as a sport," wrote Orville in 1908 for *Century* magazine. "We reluctantly entered upon the scientific side of it. But we soon found the work so fascinating that we were drawn into it deeper and deeper." Orville's statement was a bit disingenuous. They were typical entrepreneurs. As with their printing and bicycle businesses before, the thought was always in their minds that success with their "sport" could be profitable.

Wilbur's expectations probably exceeded Orville's. Wilbur sought to do something with his life that would set him apart from other men. For him, achieving powered flight became a driving ambition, not mere play. And he expected their invention of a practical flying machine to be an immediately profitable venture. He expected the American government to beat a fast path to their door with other countries close behind; he counted on private investors paying fees to use their patents; he believed they would be called upon to teach the world to fly.

The Wrights achieved powered, heavier-than-air flight in December 1903. While proving flight possible on the longest of their four flights, they had stayed in the air less than a minute, at a height of only a few feet, and covered less than one-fifth of a mile in a straight line, more or less. Both brothers understood that the 1903 Flyer was not a machine which would bring them the recognition and financial reward they expected. A practical airplane needed to be capable of sustained flight. It would have the ability to soar high enough to clear obstacles and be highly maneuverable. A practical airplane had yet to be built. But as 1903 drew to a close, the Wrights believed they could build it.

In 1904, they scaled back their bicycle business, turning the day-to-day operation over to their mechanic, Charlie Taylor, and focused all their energies on improving their aircraft and its controllability. But where work on their previous machines had been largely based on mathematical calculations and theoretical analysis, said Peter Jakab in *Visions of a Flying Machine*, improvements to the 1904 and 1905 machines were "largely trial and error."

Within days of returning from Kitty Hawk in 1903, Orville was filling his diary with plans for a new flying machine. On January 1, 1904, he sketched a muffler for the engine. On the 4th of January, he mentioned "turning the sprockets on the engine axle with a clutch." On the 7th of January, he noted that Wilbur was working on hinges, and he sketched a new valve box to hold igniter plugs. By late January, they were both working on the wood frame for the wings. In early March, Orville was finishing the engine. Finally, in April, the 1904 Flyer was ready to assemble.

Chapter Forty Three

The 1904 Flyer at Huffman Prairie

At first glance, the 1904 Flyer looked almost identical to the 1903 Flyer. Changes included an increased wing camber of 1:25 (later in the season, the camber was increased even more, to 1:30) and white pine wing spars instead of spruce. "Both alterations proved to be mistakes," said Tom Crouch in *The Bishop's Boys*. They reverted to the 1903 specifications when building their 1905 machine. The 1904 Flyer was built "heavier and stronger," said Orville some years later, making it weigh about 80 pounds more than the 1903 Flyer.

The only real improvement in the 1904 machine was the engine: This four-cylinder model was one of three they started building that winter, according to biographer Fred Kelly. It produced 16 hp—needed because of the extra weight and the lower wind speeds—and had igniters (the equivalent of spark plugs). It didn't run a whole lot smoother than their 1903 engine but it managed to keep them in the air for nearly 50 minutes in 105 attempted flights.

To overcome some of the up-and-down motion (pitch) of the nose and tail of the1903 Flyer, the Wrights carried up to 90 pounds of steel bars on the 1904 machine, changing its center of gravity. This helped but did not completely alleviate the problem. A final solution would be discovered only by making dozens of flights and spending nearly an hour in the air.

It was impractical for the Wrights to continue testing their airplanes on the Outer Banks. While the area's isolation, winds and landscape had served them well, the need for those things was past. They were able to secure the use of a 100-acre pasture owned by Torrence Huffman, the president of the Fourth National Bank of Dayton. It was 8 miles east of town at the intersection of the main roads between Dayton, Springfield and Yellow Springs. The trolley line running between Dayton and Springfield passed alongside the field. The stop was called Simms Station—that stop and Huffman Prairie are used interchangeably in the

Wrights' papers to denote the same location. Home to both cattle and horses, Huffman Prairie had been "an old swamp," Wilbur wrote in a letter to Octave Chanute. It was "filled with grassy hummocks some six inches high, so that it resembles a prairie dog town."

In the spring of 1904, Wilbur and Orville built a shed in one corner of the property and began to assemble the new Flyer. By mid-May they were ready to start flying once again.

Their flying season did not get off to a good start. The brothers were adamant about not wanting pictures of their Flyer published until patents had been secured, yet they realized their flights would be seen at Huffman Prairie and might be photographed without their consent. Deciding they might establish a *quid pro quo* with the local press, they invited all the newspapers to cover their inaugural flight (reporters were welcome; photographers were not) on May 23. Weather conditions prevented them from flying. When Wilbur offered to give a "demonstration run" down the launch track, the engine didn't perform properly.

The rest of the week's schedule is, figuratively as well as literally, cloudy. Fred Kelly, who completed his biography with the cooperation of Orville, wrote that reporters returned to Huffman Prairie "the next day" although other sources suggest it was really two days later. According to Milton Wright's diary, his sons attempted to fly again on the 25th with several reporters and other observers in attendance but, once again, they were rained out. "Many were disappointed," Milton wrote. According to Kelly, "none of those newspapermen ever returned," but other sources put two or three reporters on hand the 26th when Orville finally got off the ground for 25 feet. Some sources report Orville's first flight at Huffman Prairie took place on the 25th, although Milton's diary clearly placed it on the 26th.

Another controversy about the week's activities centers on the Wrights' intent in inviting the press. A few sources argue that Wilbur and Orville never intended to fly, believing newspapers would lose interest if they seemed unable to do what they said they could. A letter Wilbur wrote in 1906 complaining about newspaper reporters seemed to support the idea: ". . . We have already thought out a plan which we are certain will baffle such efforts as neatly as we fooled the newspapers during the two seasons we were experimenting at (Huffman Prairie)." Whatever the truth about the who, where, why and whens of that week, once the week was over, the press did not continue to cover the Wrights' flying at Huffman Prairie. According to Fred Howard in *Wilbur and Orville,* "Deliberate or not, the failure of the Wrights to fly in the presence of reporters . . . worked like a charm. It would be sixteen months before another reporter set foot on Huffman Prairie."

It was just as well. For most of the summer, the brothers struggled to get their airplane into the air. Once in the air, partly due to slow launch speeds, they had trouble keeping it there. Some flights never got off the ground; those that did ended before going very far.

Launching the machine was the Wrights' biggest challenge in 1904. Winds at Huffman Prairie in spring and summer were light (often well under the 11 mph they needed), requiring a longer run to reach takeoff speed. The Wrights lengthened their launch track to 160 then 240 feet (from 60 feet used in 1903) but often it was still not enough. The plane needed to take off into the wind and that posed another problem: Winds at Huffman Prairie were erratic. They would often get the track laid in one direction only to find the wind was coming from another. It was "back-breaking work," reported Crouch. They either had "to begin all over again, or risk the dangers of a crosswind takeoff."

In early September, they revived an idea they had tried on a smaller scale at Kitty Hawk back in 1900. They built a 20-foot derrick to help launch the Flyer. Stationed at the head of the rail, the derrick was armed with a 1,600-pound weight that dropped 16.5 feet to produce 350 pounds of pull through a system of pulleys and gears. The device made it possible to safely launch the plane from a 60-foot rail in very light winds.

The derrick made an immediate difference in their success. According to Howard, Wilbur made the first 10 starts with the device and "seven resulted in true flights." Later that month, he flew a complete circle, covering over 4,000 feet in one minute, 36 seconds. In November, "he circled the field four times in five minutes, landing only when the Flyer's engine showed signs of overheating." Less than a month later,

Orville matched Wilbur's performance.

After solving the launch problem, the Wrights continued to have trouble. Landings were often little more than crashes. Down-time for repairs ran into weeks. Octave Chanute visited Dayton to see them fly in October, but Orville's first demonstration was short and the landing hard. It took three days to repair the damage. Chanute had to leave before the plane was able to fly again.

In spite of the problems, the Wrights succeeded in improving control of the machine before their flying season ended on December 9. "We finished our experiments several weeks ago," wrote Wilbur to Chanute on December 20. "We succeeded in curing the trouble caused by the tendency of the machine to turn up too much laterally when a short turn was made."

The time had come for them to "reap whatever reward they could obtain from their invention," wrote Harry Combs in *Kill Devil Hill*. They didn't have a practical flying machine yet but they were close. While they began making plans for a new Flyer, they also devoted time to securing their patents and marketing their invention of powered flight.

Chapter Forty Four

U.S. government turns Wrights down

In early 1905, the Wrights wrote to their congressman, asking him if the U. S. War Department would be interested in their invention. The congressman forwarded their letter to the War Department. The Wrights' inquiry must not have been the first received concerning airplanes. The department's response read like a bad form letter. Although the Wrights did not mention money, they were advised that the War Department was making no allocations for "experimental development of devices for mechanical flight." They were also told their machine could not be considered because it "has not yet been brought to the state of practical operation."

The Wrights tried again in October and were turned down once again with almost the same wording. "The Government would not be interested until after the machine had been brought to the stage of practical operation." Considering they had completed nearly two hundred flights in their machine, some more than 30 minutes in duration, the response was absurd.

But, as Crouch points out: "The Wrights had not included any photos . . . nor provided letters from eyewitnesses. In fact, they offered no proof at all, only the bald assertion that their machine worked. To expect a positive response from the War Department on that basis indicates Wilbur and Orville's inability to understand and deal effectively with a government bureaucracy."

After the first brush-off from the U.S. War Department, the Wrights offered their flying machine to the British War Office and were told a military attaché would call on them.

Chapter Forty Five

The 1905 Flyer

It took two years of trial-and-error before the Wrights had what they considered a "machine of practical utility." Although 1904 had been frustrating and not as productive as they hoped, what the Wrights learned from the experience was a necessary part of the process of invention.

The question of how much power an airplane needed to be practical weighed heavily on Wilbur's mind after the 1904 flying season. Clearly a plane that couldn't fly without 15 mph winds or better—or one that needed a launching tower to catapult it into the air—had limited value. The question was also worrying Octave Chanute at the end of the year. "I have now a curiosity to know what are your final conclusions as to the power actually required for artificial flight, and whether you hope to reduce it. I am under the impression that birds use less power than you have found necessary," he wrote.

Wilbur, who loved an investigative challenge, pursued Chanute's line of questioning, catching birds and measuring them to determine just how much power they did use. "After considering its structure and its flight," he wrote about a 14 oz. crow he captured in late February 1905, "I am far from believing that it expends less power, in proportion to weight and speed, than is readily attainable in a dynamic flying machine of large size." The argument between the two men continued through April.

"I see no hope, based on any information at present accessible, for any considerable advance on what we have already done in the matter of dynamic efficiency," Wilbur wrote to Chanute. " I think the great room for improvement will be found to be in mechanical details and methods, and especially in the skill of the operators." Later that season, his conclusion was borne out.

The Wrights began assembling the 1905 Flyer in late May. Reverting to the spruce used in all their machines up to 1904, they set out to build a stronger machine frame that wouldn't break apart with every hard landing. These measures added about 25 pounds to the weight of the frame.

Camber of the wings was returned to 1:20, a move that helped the machine take off at slower speeds. To help control stalling (an ongoing problem even today with inexperienced pilots), they eventually adjusted the wing design to have less angle at the tips than in the center. They kept the wider, thinner propeller design of 1904, but added a sweeping backwards curve to retain the propeller shape under pressure in flight.

"The most radical change was the addition of two semi-circular vanes, called 'blinkers,'" explained Kelly. These vanes "entirely removed the danger of tail spinning" but "added to the difficulty of steering, both when flying straight and when making turns."

"The controls of the 1905 machine were operated in a slightly different manner from those of the 1903 machine. The vertical rear rudder was not connected up . . . to automatically operate in conjunction with the wing- warping, but instead was coupled to a lever, so that it could be operated either independently of the warping or in conjunction therewith. It was operated in this manner in a few of the flights in 1904 but not in many . . . ," Orville recalled in *How We Invented the Airplane.*

Only the propulsion system (motor, propellers and chain drive) from the 1904 machine was reused. The motor, which had started the 1904 season coughing and stalling, now—after hours of operation in the air and on the ground—ran smoothly, produced 20 hp and was capable of flying at 35 mph.

The final machine had a wingspan of 40.5 feet and was 28 feet long, 9.5 feet high. It weighed about 850 pounds, some 65 pounds lighter than the 1904 Flyer (after the 1904 machine was loaded with its steel bar ballast). The Wrights estimated it had adequate water and fuel for an hour of flying time although, later in the season, after running out of gas, they tripled the size of the one-gallon fuel tank.

While the 1905 Flyer was under construction, the Wrights worried about protecting their invention. They were expecting the British attaché any day—and if an agreement couldn't be reached with him, they had reason to believe the French might be interested. "We have felt serious misgivings regarding the advisability of any further experiments prior to reaching an understanding with some government," Wilbur wrote to

Chanute on May 28. "At present our machine is a complete secret, but it may not remain so if we attempt further experiments, like those of last year."

After hearing nothing more from the British, the Wrights rolled out the 1905 Flyer and began test flights on June 23. Over the next several weeks, Wilbur's diary documents the flights made and the continuing control problems. Finally, a crash on July 14 with Orville operating the machine provided the incentive to make more changes. The front horizontal elevator area was increased from 53 to 83 square feet and moved twice the distance from the front of the wings (from 7.3 to 11.7 feet) lengthening the control lever. This additional distance gave the operator more leeway. Where an inch up or down with the shorter lever caused drastic shifts, the same movement with the longer lever made only small adjustments. At some point, they eliminated the "droop" of the wings, useful in the higher crosswinds of the Outer Banks but unnecessary in Ohio.

In a letter to Chanute a couple days after Orville's crash, Wilbur wrote: "We have made several changes in the operating handles and have had some trouble instantly acquiring familiarity with them. We are sure they will be a good thing when we have learned the combination properly."

"The aircraft that emerged differed significantly from that of a few weeks before. It embodied all they knew about flying—and some educated guesses. Back in the air on August 24, an enormous improvement in performance was immediately apparent," said Crouch.

Later in August they made a couple more adjustments, improving the lateral control of the machine by enlarging the biplane rear vertical rudder from a total of 20 square feet to 34. They moved the rear rudder out 3 more feet from the back of the wings.

Toward the end of September more local people began to take note of the flying activity at Huffman Prairie. No one had really noticed in 1904 because the flights were all short (most under one minute) and none made it more than 15 feet off the ground. Now the Wrights were flying 5, 10, 15 minutes or more at a time and at altitudes up to 60 feet. The longest flight, with Wilbur at the controls, was made October 5. He flew 24 miles in 39 minutes, 24 seconds. These flights were much harder to ignore. Although the crowds were small, word traveled fast. The Wrights, still worried about keeping their machine a secret, decided to stop flying and concentrate on getting the machine sold.

"Some friends whom we unwisely permitted to witness some of the flights could not keep silent, and on the evening of the 5th the *Daily News* had an article. . . . " wrote Wilbur to Chanute on October 16. "Consequently we are doing nothing at present, but before the season closes we wish to go out someday and make an effort to put the record above one hour." Whatever his intentions, Wilbur went to Huffman Prairie late that same day and made one final flight in the 1905 Flyer. He circled the field in just over one minute and landed. The season was over. They had made 50 flights, spending 216 minutes in the air.

More importantly, they had found the "final piece to the control puzzle," Wilbur said some years later. It concerned lateral control of the machine while circling. "The remedy was found to consist in more the skillful operation of the machine and not in a different construction.... When we had discovered the real nature of the trouble, and knew that it could always be remedied . . . we felt that we were ready to place flying machines on the market."

Chapter Forty Six

Selling a well-kept secret proves difficult

After the brothers built and flew what they considered their first practical airplane, they should have been poised for success. Articles about
their first flights appeared in a number of scientific journals. They had
been invited to exhibit their plane at the upcoming St. Louis Exposition,
and they were corresponding with dozens of other aviation pioneers
around the world. Instead, the Wrights were discouraged by their own
government's lack of interest, and were frantically seeking a market.
They sent letters to contacts they had made in the British government and
in France. If the United States didn't want their flying machine, they were
certain someone else would.

The Royal Aeronautical Society in England was particularly interested in what the Wrights were doing and published several laudatory but
vague reports of their progress. The British War Office took note, too. In
October 1904, Colonel John Edward Capper had been sent to Dayton to
visit the Wrights.

But the Wrights were not about to share their secrets with anyone.
They had been secretive all along, and now they became even more so,
convinced that others would steal their ideas and profit from their invention. Capper was not allowed to see their plane "in the air or on the
ground," according to historian Alfred Gollin in *No Longer an Island*.
"Despite their caution and vigilance, [the Wrights] showed [Capper]
every courtesy. They spoke to him at some length about their experiments; they permitted him to examine one of their motors; and they
allowed him to see several photographs of their aircraft in flight." Capper
was impressed and asked that Great Britain be given "the first chance" to
buy their machine, said Wilbur later. "We told him that we were not yet
ready to talk business." Three months later, after being turned away by
the U.S. government the first time, they opened negotiations with the
British who had an immediate need for a reliable flying machine.

At the turn of the century, Great Britain's mighty empire was begin-

ning to crumble. Other nations coveted some of Britain's prized posses-
sions and helped foment native unrest. And after years of observing the
disparities between Anglo-Saxons and themselves, the natives were rest-
less on their own. The problems of managing governments and populations in every corner of the world were taking their toll. As life heading
into the 20th century sped up, populations spread into harder-to-reach
inland areas of Australia, Africa, India and other continents. Europe itself
was forming alliances across its land borders in which England, as an
island, could not share. Naval superiority, once England's ace-in-the-
hole, was no longer enough to secure her borders—at home or abroad.
Great Britain realized early on that air power might solve some of its
problems. As early as 1894, the British government was investigating
military uses for kites, balloons and gliders. By the time the Wrights flew
at Kitty Hawk in 1903, the British were already committed to developing
military aircraft.

Aviation enthusiasts in England and Europe had been seriously pursuing manned flight but were making little progress toward powered
flight in heavier-than-air craft. The use of gliders and kites—two forms
of flight with longer documented histories—was considered risky as
proved by the deaths of several promising aviators at the end of the
1800s. Balloons were unreliable and often uncontrollable but had proved,
so far, to be the only practical form of military air transport. Britain had
established an aviation facility at Aldershot, England, under the auspices
of its War Office. "Despite its archaic name the Balloon Factory, by 1904,
was involved in all forms of aerial activity," wrote Gollin.

In spite of Capper's initial enthusiasm for the Wrights, he had a hard
time convincing his superiors in the British War Office, which (like the
U.S. military) had already received hundreds of solicitations for all sorts
of flying schemes that never materialized. Many British officials had
convinced themselves that man's destiny in the sky was the powered balloon or dirigible. Widely publicized progress was being made with
lighter-than-air flight.

The Wrights, on the other hand, continued to shroud their work in
secrecy, declining the invitation to exhibit their plane at the St. Louis

Exposition and refusing to demonstrate their capabilities to any potential customer without a signed contract. The lengthy proposal they submitted to the British after months of intermittent negotiations was criticized by one historian as "philosophical rigamarole." Even Gollin, a sympathetic biographer, admitted it was an "unusual and extraordinary set of offers."

It may be that the British, as interested as they were in gaining air superiority, didn't know what to make of the Wrights and their way of doing business. If so, they were the first in a line of several potential customers who had difficulty coming to terms with the Ohio brothers. The British acknowledged receipt of the proposal and then did nothing.

Chapter Forty Seven

Finagling with the French

As young men, Wilbur and Orville had run a printing business and published several community newspapers. Wilbur had proved himself to be a skillful marketer, planning creative promotions, blanketing the neighborhood with flyers and using other methods to attract attention and sell their products. But now, less than 20 years later, Wilbur was trying to make a far more difficult sale while breaking all the rules of good marketing. Fearful that someone would steal and profit from their ideas, he chose to conduct their flying experiments away from the public eye, refused to publish detailed reports of their work or take part in aeronautical exhibitions. He expected potential buyers to commit $200,000 or more (a huge sum in 1905) sight unseen for something most men could not even imagine. It proved to be too great a leap of faith for all but the most astute aeronautical engineers of his day.

Capt. Ferdinand Ferber, one of France's leading aviation experts, was one of the few men who believed in the Wrights' capabilities. A long time correspondent of Octave Chanute, he published an article in *L'Aérophile* in 1903 that, according to British aviation historian Charles Gibbs-Smith, "was the first clarion-call on behalf of aviation," directed at the French aeronautical community warning of America's imminent superiority. Acknowledging that European aviation was focused on balloons and lighter-than-air craft, Ferber urged the French to follow Lilienthal's example and change their focus to heavier-than-air flight.

There was little response to Ferber's article until it was underscored by Chanute in an address to the *Aéro-Club de France* just two months later. Americans were poised to surpass the French in the air, according to Chanute, who described the Wrights' successful gliding experiments. After Chanute's lecture, Ferber wrote to French flying enthusiast Ernest Archdeacon. And Archdeacon, a wealthy and influential attorney, began fanning the flames of French nationalism.

Count Henry de La Vaulx described Archdeacon's reaction in his

1911 history of aviation: "Anxious to keep for his country the glory of seeing born the first man-carrying aeroplane which would raise itself from the ground by its own power . . . Ernest Archdeacon decided to shake our aviators out of their torpor and put a stop to the indifference of French opinion concerning flying machines."

Archdeacon began with an article in *La Locomotion,* warning that the French were being eclipsed by the Americans when it came to heavier-than-air flight. "Will the homeland of Montgolfier (inventor of the hot air balloon) have the shame of allowing this ultimate discovery of aerial science—which is certainly imminent, and which will constitute the greatest scientific revolution that has been since the beginning of the world—to be realized abroad?" he wrote. The article was reprinted in *L'Aérophile.* That the glory of manned flight should fall to another country was not a possibility the French took lightly.

News of the Wrights' first powered flights was reported in France at about the same time and with as much inaccuracy as it was in America. Wilbur was given credit for flying more than 3 miles, at a height of more than 65 feet, in a plane powered by a tricycle engine, after being launched from the top of Kill Devil Hill. The French—like almost anyone who heard the news but had yet to see an airplane fly—were skeptical. When the true facts of the first flights finally emerged a month later (the plane flew less than a minute, covering less than one fifth of a mile, at a height of just 8 to 10 feet), the French shrugged off the report. "The experiment is not as grand as we thought," wrote Ferber to Archdeacon.

Victor Tatin, a respected French aviation pioneer, was reported in the February issue of *L'Aérophile* to be "somewhat skeptical" because the reports were so "incomplete and often contradictory. . . . In any case," he said, " the problem cannot be considered as completely solved by the mere fact of someone having flown for less than a minute."

Archdeacon, in an address to the *Aéro-Club* in February 1904 acknowledged that the Wrights "have pushed much farther ahead in this kind of study than we have." But, echoing Tatin's contention that the Wrights' flights did not really prove anything, he went on: "We are, however, exceptionally well placed to succeed, since we are the real fathers of the light motor. . . . We must hurry if we wish to catch up to the enormous advance made over us by the Americans."

"If we continue, we shall rapidly catch up with—and even overtake the Americans," he rallied, pleading for subscribers to help defray the cost of this race. "It is absolutely essential to ensure for France the glory of the ultimate conquest of the air."

The Wrights, of course, believed credit for the conquest of the air already belonged to them. They stepped into the middle of this one-sided rivalry in 1905 when they wrote to Ferber, as mutual friends of Chanute's, asking if the French government would be interested in purchasing their airplane.

Ferber and the Wrights shared a respect for Otto Lilienthal and the belief that powered flight would only be achieved after the theory and mechanics of free flight were mastered. Ferber had in fact published a tribute to the Wrights' work earlier in 1905, announcing that they had flown for more than five minutes and been able to maneuver their machine in a circular flight path. Even so, details about their machine and flight were so scarce that even Ferber didn't grasp the full significance of what they had already achieved.

Ferber passed the Wrights' letter on to the head of balloon and airship research for the French army, along with his opinion that the Wrights' proposal was worth considering. The army was particularly keen to succeed in the air. National pride as inventors of the hot air balloon was at stake. On a more practical level the French were lagging behind the Germans and British. Having command of the air might swing the balance of power back their way.

Shortly after writing to Ferber—and after finally realizing that a little publicity might help their cause—the Wrights sent a letter describing their 1905 flying experiments to aeronautical leaders in Great Britain, France and Germany. Even though they already held patents in France and Germany for their airplane, the letter didn't explain how they achieved controlled flight. Instead, it described a machine under the control of an operator, capable of flying dozens of miles, flying in circles and performing other controlled feats heretofore undoable.

The letter was published in two widely read French journals, and it set off a furor of accusations and disbelief. The definition of flying was still very much up in the air, so to speak. The French controversy raised numerous questions. Did a plane fly if it had to be launched into the air rather than lifting off the ground under its own power? There were rumors that the Wrights' flying machine had to be catapulted into the air: Was that flight? How far and how long did a machine have to travel before it achieved flight? Reports of the Wrights' first flights staked their success on feet rather than miles, on air times measured in seconds rather than minutes. Of what practical use was this?

Archdeacon, whose efforts to meet the Wrights and see their flying machine in Dayton earlier in the year had been rebuffed, led the challenge: "Whatever respect I feel for the Wrights—whose first experiments without a motor are undeniable and of the greatest interest—it is impossible for me to accept as historical truth the report of their latest tests," he said in an address to the *Fédération Aéronautique Internationale*. The Americans might be on to something, but real flight had yet to be achieved. France still had the chance to lead the world into the air. Many of Archdeacon's peers agreed.

But Ferber, who knew somewhat more about the science of flight than Archdeacon, believed the Wrights held the key to success. Ferber had first hand knowledge. Between 1902 and 1905, he built two gliders based on what limited information he had about the Wrights' design. Although historian Charles Gibb-Smith called the Ferber-Wright glider "a somewhat pathetic contraption, and primitive to a degree," the glider worked better than any other design Ferber had tried. He considered it a success.

In spite of Archdeacon's professed skepticism, Ferber contacted him, hoping to win his approval for the idea that France might buy the Wrights' machine, copy its design and be the first world power to control the skies. Archdeacon would have none of it. "M. Archdeacon declares that he persists in believing that the machine is still only tentative. . . ." wrote the editor of *L'Aérophile*.

Although the French army had told the Wrights they were interested in making a purchase, Ferber believed such a deal was unlikely. The asking price of a million francs raised eyebrows among the military hierarchy and several of his well-connected peers—especially Archdeacon—publicly declared their disbelief in the Wrights' claims."

Ferber pulled together a small syndicate of French investors willing to spend a million francs to obtain the machine. The syndicate included Ferber and M. Henri Letellier, publisher of a Paris newspaper. "These gentlemen planned to purchase a Wright machine as a gift to the nation," wrote Crouch in *The Bishop's Boys*, "in return for which they expected nothing more than the gratitude of their countrymen—and perhaps the Legion of Honor."

The syndicate sent Letellier's secretary, Arnold Fordyce, to negotiate a contract with the Wrights. Every circumstance of the deal seems fantastic if judged by today's business standards. There were no credit checks, no references, no red tape. The Frenchman simply showed up with a letter of introduction in Dayton aiming to purchase one of the most important pieces of technology in the history of the world. The Wrights weren't even certain who Fordyce represented, "but they have some strange ways in France," wrote Wilbur to Chanute, "and we did not wish to be caught napping." Ferber had told the Wrights that Fordyce was a "friend." Some historians also claim Ferber implied Fordyce represented the government because he assumed (correctly) that the Wrights preferred to sell the machine to a government. In any case, Wilbur and Chanute exchanged several letters before Fordyce arrived in Dayton and Chanute offered his belief "that the 'friend'. . . is really an agent of the French war department, which sends him as an individual in order to 'save face' if you turn out to be a 'bluff.'"

Fordyce arrived at the Wrights' home in Dayton on Thursday, December 28, 1905, and "was quick to correct the misunderstanding," according to Crouch. By December 30, they reached an agreement that gave the syndicate an option to purchase one Wright Flyer, with the stipulation that the machine had to be turned over to the French military. "Wilbur and Orville sign up the contract with Mr. Arnold Fordyce of Paris, to furnish a flyer, etc. for One Million Francs," wrote Milton

Wright in his diary that night.

For the French equivalent of $200,000, the Wrights would have to demonstrate that the plane could fly at least 30 miles in one hour, train one pilot and disclose their "secret" data which the French assumed would allow them to duplicate the Wrights' success in airplane design. The Wrights had offered exclusive rights to their airplane but, of course, such exclusivity came at a much higher price. The French, who still believed they would be making substantial improvements to the Wrights' design and producing their own planes, weren't interested.

The Wrights were disappointed that no country realized the advantage of being the only country with air power. Not only would that have validated the universal importance of their invention, but they believed if one government alone controlled the air, that the airplane would be an effective deterrent to war. Chanute, who for years had preached that powered flight would put an end to war, encouraged this view. "I still adhere to my original belief that the best disposal of your machine would be to have it go to one single government who would keep it secret and thus promote peace. . . ." he wrote to Wilbur in December 1905.

"The idea of selling to a single government as a strict secret has some advantages," responded Wilbur, "but we are very much disinclined to assume the moral responsibility of choosing the proper one which we have no means of knowing how it will use the invention."

It was a moral issue which the Wrights acknowledged but over which they probably lost no sleep. Through the years, as airplanes proved far better at wreaking destruction than preserving peace, Orville never expressed any regret for his role.

And in 1905 when the downside of powered flight was far from anyone's thought, the Wrights were focused on selling their invention. It had been five years since they began their quest to fly in earnest, and they had yet to earn a penny for their efforts.

Chapter Forty Eight

Ups and downs

As the year 1905 drew to a close, Wilbur and Orville believed they were on the verge of earning their reward for inventing a practical airplane. They had just signed their first sales contract, giving the group of French investors an option to buy one plane. The French hadn't wanted to pay for exclusive rights, so the brothers were free to sell their invention to anyone else willing to make a deal.

The contract with the French guaranteed to put money into the Wrights' hands. They had already built a machine that would uphold their part of the bargain. If the French decided not to exercise their option, the Wrights would earn $5,000 for their trouble. As it turned out, they got their $5,000—but didn't sell an airplane for four more years.

The French syndicate signed the contract without seeing the Wrights' machine fly but soon turned the contract over to the French military. Government officials were unwilling to gamble $200,000 on something they'd never seen. They also had second thoughts about turning down exclusive rights to the machine, but the Wrights initially refused to renegotiate. Although the Wrights later changed their minds and agreed to the revised terms, the French option lapsed.

The Wrights tried to reopen negotiations with the British and hit the same stumbling block: Each government interested in the Wrights' plane had already backed unsuccessful flying schemes. Political reality required that any new endeavor be proven practical before new contracts were signed. But the Wrights had packed their airplane away and weren't showing it to anyone.

In spite of their ability to think outside the box when it came to machinery, the Wrights were particularly obtuse when it came to marketing their airplane. Seeing themselves as honorable men, they believed their proposed contract provided all the protection from fraud a potential buyer needed. If their airplane didn't perform as promised, the contract would be void and any deposit refunded. From a legal standpoint, they

were probably correct; from a public relations point of view, they could-
n't have been more wrong. The British once again backed away from a
deal with the Wrights.

At the end of 1906, the Wrights had no prospects for direct sales.
With patents for their invention in place in overseas markets, they began
negotiating with a New York investment firm, Charles R. Flint & Co., for
the foreign rights to their machine. Within a few months, they worked out
a deal allowing Flint to serve as their European agent.

About the same time, publicity generated by their negotiations with
the British and French finally paid off at home. The United States "could
no longer assign aeronautics to the pigeonhole in which it had been
allowed to languish since Langley's Aerodrome splashed into the
Potomac in 1903," wrote biographer Fred Howard in *Wilbur and Orville*.
Encouraged by President Theodore Roosevelt and his Secretary of War,
and soon-to-be-president, William Howard Taft, the military began making inquiries among America's nascent aviation community. "We
received a communication from the U.S. Board of Ordnance &
Fortification notifying us that the Board had under consideration several
propositions for the construction and testing of flying machines," wrote
Wilbur to Chanute in May 1907.

Within a week of receiving the board's letter, Orville replied. "We
have some flyers in course of construction, and would be pleased to sell
one or more of them to the War Department, if an agreement as to terms
can be reached." Orville's letter was short and to the point: "These
machines will carry two men, an operator and an observer, and a suffi-
cient supply of fuel for a flight of two hundred kilometers. We are willing to make it a condition of a contract that the machine must make a trial
trip before Government representatives of not less than fifty kilometers at
a speed of not less than fifty kilometers an hour, before its acceptance by
the Department, and before any part of the purchase price is paid to us."

The Wrights offered to meet with department representatives to discuss the matter "in detail," he said, "or we are willing to submit a formal
proposition." Although he didn't say so, they had no intention of demonstrating their machine for the Americans either.

In June at the request of the board, the Wrights submitted a formal proposal, asking the War Department for $100,000 to cover the cost of an airplane and the training to fly it. The military also raised the question of exclusive rights to the machine. When told an existing contract made that impossible, "the door [to a sale] seemed to have been quietly closed again," wrote Howard. In fact, the door wasn't closed; it was swinging open very slowly.

The Wrights received a response to their proposal in October. Their asking price of $100,000 was too steep, but the board was interested in further negotiations and wanted to meet with them Based on earlier attempts to interest the board in their machine, the brothers were skeptical. "We are not sanguine that the Board is really in a mood to reach an agreement, but we will give the matter serious attention," Wilbur had written when the board first made contact. This new response was encouraging. Selling their flying machine to the Americans had always been the Wrights' preference. They now determined to do whatever it would take to make this happen.

The War Department's latest inquiry had reached the brothers while they were in Europe doing business with their new international sales agent, Flint and Co.. Wilbur had traveled to London in late May and from there to Paris. The French, working through a private consortium on behalf of the government, had allowed their 1905 option to purchase the Wright plane to lapse. Flint believed the deal could be resurrected through a different group of financiers. According to Crouch, Wilbur pushed to deal directly with the French government. Neither approach was productive. The French government kept changing its contract demands while rivalries and misunderstandings doomed the private syndicate.

Until Orville arrived in France in late July, the situation was made worse by delays on the Wrights' part. The brothers had agreed they both would approve all provisions of the contract, but Orville seemed to balk on a few key issues. Letters took weeks to travel back and forth; cables were limited to telegraph short-speak. Relations between the two were strained. By early July, their letters were full of recriminations. "I have had only one letter a week from you (these very short)," wrote Orville on

July 11. "I have practically no information of what is going on. When you cable, you never explain anything so that I can answer with any certainly that we are talking about the same thing. . . . You have not answered a single question I had asked. . . . "

When Wilbur's father, Milton, also complained about the quality of his correspondence, Wilbur replied testily, "The complaint that I have not written fully and promptly is incomprehensible to me. . . . You people in Dayton seem to me to be very lacking in perspicacity."

Wilbur, believing a contract with the French was finally imminent in mid-July, instructed that an airplane be shipped to France. He asked Orville to join him. Within a few days of Orville's arrival in Paris, the two hammered out a new proposal for the French government. The exact details have been omitted from the published papers and biographies of the Wrights. At the least, the contract met the provisions of an earlier proposal: six months exclusive use of an airplane capable of flying 50 kilometers at altitudes up to 300 meters for one million francs.

After submitting the French proposal and receiving no response, Wilbur and Hart Berg, the Flint and Co. agent in Europe, left for Berlin to talk with the Germans. The Germans, who up to this point had invested most of their efforts in lighter-than-air flight (balloons and dirigibles), may have been seriously interested in the Wrights' plane. But like everyone else the Wrights dealt with, they wanted to see it fly. By late September, the Germans had told Wilbur they couldn't make a commitment without flying trials. Wilbur wasn't ready to make that concession. He headed home, planning to give the Germans another shot at the plane in 1908.

In the middle of negotiating with the Germans, Wilbur and Orville submitted another new proposal to the French that went nowhere. "We finally concluded that the French were not in proper spirit to receive such a proposition and finally on Aug. 24 (1907) sent a letter to the Minister of War . . . withdrawing all offers," wrote Wilbur in his journal.

Chapter Forty Nine

Back to the U.S.

Wilbur went to Europe in May 1907 and spent the next six months trying to sell his airplane to the French and the Germans. He returned to the United States in November without a contract from either country. It had been nearly four years since he and Orville proved man could fly at Kitty Hawk—and the brothers still hadn't sold a single airplane or turned a profit from their invention.

Wilbur was not often optimistic about his prospects in life. But throughout the years he and Orville struggled to find a market for their flying machine, he remained confident that contracts would be signed and that their hard work would be rewarded. Because Great Britain, France and Germany had active, government-supported aeronautical programs and all had shown serious interest in the Wrights' airplane, he had believed that the best possibility for sales existed outside the United States.

The United States government had seemed clueless about what the Wrights had accomplished. Even so, at the end of 1907, it suddenly became a better prospect. "If we can obtain assurances that we shall receive fair treatment . . . we on our part will make every reasonable concession in order to provide a basis of agreement which it will be possible for your Board to accept," wrote Orville to the U.S. Board of Ordnance and Fortification on October 30. "We care much more for an assurance of fair treatment than for an extreme price on the first machine. . . . During the past eighteen months all of our offers to foreign governments have contained provisions giving us liberty to furnish machines to our own government absolutely without restriction. Nothing would give us greater pleasure than to furnish the first machine to it," he continued. "If this matter interests your Board one of us will return to America for a conference at once. . . . "

Wilbur didn't wait for a response. He left Liverpool, England, aboard the *"R.M.S. Baltic"* on November 11. After arriving in New York 11 days later, he traveled to Washington before heading back to Dayton. On November 25, 1907, Wilbur sat down for the first time with representatives from the U.S. government. He offered to sell the first airplane to the U.S. government for $25,000, a quarter of their original asking price. "They have some experiment money and would probably appropriate $10,000 immediately to the purchase of one of our machines," wrote Wilbur to Orville after returning to Dayton. "They might give more but I think they would hesitate to go as high as twenty-five thousand." To pay $25,000, the board would have to request an appropriation from Congress, Wilbur explained. "No appropriation could be available before March."

Today's bureaucracy is nothing new. At the turn of the 20th century, it was a vast network of political influence, tempered by democratic ideals, grinding along in ways not unfamiliar 100 years later. Both cumbersome and conservative as bureaucracies tend to be, U.S. military officials spent four years ignoring what the Wright brothers accomplished at Kitty Hawk in 1903. Their interest was only whetted when American newspapers began reporting that the British, French and German governments were all considering the purchase of Wright airplanes.

Now that the U.S. War Department was suitably motivated to buy an airplane, the Wrights had little trouble coming to terms with them by the end of year. But the barriers to closing the deal were no different from what they would be today. Even with the money in hand, the department couldn't stroke a check for $25,000. They first needed to advertise for competitive bids. The contract, of course, would have to be awarded to the lowest bidder.

A solicitation for bids for the construction of an airplane was advertised, based on what Wilbur told the board the Wright Flyer could do. Those specifications, according to biographer Fred Kelly in *The Wright Brothers*, required a machine that could carry a pilot and passenger, "weighing not less than 350 lbs.," average 40 mph in a 10-mile test and "carry enough fuel for 125 miles." The plane had to remain aloft for at least one hour, land without damage, and "must be built in such a way that it could be taken apart, and later reassembled, without too much difficulty, when necessary to transport it on an army truck from one place to another."

The Wrights knew they could build the plane the army wanted. Because no known person in the entire world had come close to matching their flying performance at Huffman Prairie in 1904 and 1905, they expected to be the only bidders—an assumption the War Department shared. In accordance with their informal agreement with the government, the Wrights submitted their bid on January 27, 1908, for $25,000, promising delivery of a plane for field trials within 200 days. Much to everyone's surprise, theirs wasn't the only bid.

"In fact," reported Crouch, "there were forty-one proposals. . . . They ranged in price from a bargain-basement $850 to $1 million." Some of the bids were immediately disqualified. Others were eliminated when the required 10 percent bond was not posted. Three bids remained.

One of the remaining three, a bid of $1,000 for a plane to be built in 185 days by a Chicago man who, as yet, had never built or flown a plane, was withdrawn. The second bid, for $20,000 with a delivery time of 180 days, was from Augustus Herring. Herring, a former associate of Langley and Chanute, was well known in aeronautical circles. At Chanute's invitation, he had visited the Wrights at Kitty Hawk in 1902 and conducted brief experiments with his own glider while there. The War Department considered Herring a legitimate contender although the Wrights were quite certain he could not fulfill his contract. They were correct. After several delays and bombastic press conferences, Herring withdrew his proposal to concentrate on more lucrative "private" business. He never built an airplane that could fly.

Chapter Fifty

Racing the clock

The final success of manned flight after centuries of failure was not attributable to any one single thing. Powered manned flight needed a means for both horizontal and lateral control, a lightweight power source and an understanding of aeronautic principles that until the late 18th century, had yet to be clearly defined.

Although men had tried many wing configurations, by the time Wilbur and Orville Wright came along, many experiments already pointed to the fixed bi-wing for horizontal stability. By the late 1800s, engineers were hard at work reducing the weight and increasing the horsepower of steam and gasoline engines. Without the burgeoning automobile industry, powered flight never would have gotten off the ground.

So when the Wrights set to work in 1900 at Kitty Hawk, the one piece of the powered flight puzzle yet to be solved was lateral control. Their solution, wing-warping, was one of several possible solutions. It may not have been the best solution. It just happened to be the first—combined with all the other "right" pieces—that worked.

Any credible historian today gives the Wrights their well-deserved due: They put the pieces together and flew first. Their unexpected success spurred the process of invention as most (if not all) major breakthroughs in technology have done. On the heels of first flight, others began revising, reworking, and rethinking powered flight and in a few short years pushed the technology beyond the Wrights' wildest dreams.

According to Pulitzer Prize winner Jared Diamond in *Guns, Germs and Steel*, history has typically overstated the importance of "genius" inventors. History would not have been altered significantly if the Wrights had not been born in a particular place and time, he suggests. "All recognized famous inventors had capable predecessors and successors. . . . My two main conclusions are that technology develops cumulatively, rather than in isolated heroic acts."

Octave Chanute, America's leading student—and promoter—of

aeronautical invention at the time the Wrights entered the field, voiced the same belief a century before Diamond. But the Wrights for all their intuitive genius, couldn't see the truth in it. In October 1906, Wilbur wrote to Chanute that their lack of concern about competition in the air was "not a question of relative ability, but of mathematical probabilities."

"The world does not contain greater men than Maxim, Bell, Edison, Langley, Lilienthal, & Chanute. We are not so foolish as to base our belief upon any supposed superiority to these men and to all those who will hereafter take up the problem. If the wheels of time could be turned back six years, it is not at all probable that we would do again what we have done. . . . It was due to a peculiar combination of circumstances which might never occur again," Wilbur explained.

But Chanute urged the brothers to get their machines sold, even if it meant taking less money than they wanted. Wilbur continued to insist they were in no hurry. "If it were true that others would be flying within a year or two, there would be reason in selling at any price but we are convinced that no one will be able to develop a practical flyer within five years. This opinion is based on cold calculation. It takes into consideration practical and scientific difficulties whose existence is unknown to all but ourselves," wrote Wilbur.

"When we see men laboring year after year on points we overcame within a few weeks, without ever getting far enough along to meet the worse point beyond, we know that their rivalry and competition is not to be feared for many years. When the distance is known and the speed is known a reasonable estimate of the time required can be formed. It is many times five years. We do not believe there is one chance in a hundred that anyone will have a machine of the least practical usefulness within five years."

Chanute was unconvinced. "I suppose that you realize that Esnault-Pelterie, Ferber, Blériot & Voisin, Barlatier & Blanc, Vuia, Cornu, Cody and a German syndicate are also all experimenting with dynamic flying machines," responded Chanute a few days later.

Over the next year, Chanute continued to pepper the Wrights with news reports about competing flyers. In January 1908 Wilbur wrote, "I note from several remarks in your recent letters that you evidently view the present situation in aviation circles with very different eyes from what we do. I must confess that I still hold to my prediction that an independent solution of the flying problem would require at least five years."

Wilbur's confidence was strengthened by the various patents the Wrights had filed in the United States, Great Britain, France and Germany. In his view, without wing-warping and other features affecting "automatic control" covered by these patents, sustained practical flight was not possible. "We do not believe it will be found easy to construct machines comparing in quality with ours without palpable infringement of our claims." wrote Wilbur to Chanute later that spring.

It's doubtful that Wilbur believed his success in flight was simple chance although as a man who respected predictable science his belief in the law of probability is not out of the question. Most likely, he saw himself as an instrument of some greater destiny. It is not unusual to find such ego in men whose accomplishments have outstripped their peers. Wilbur, not known as a boastful man, thought he was simply stating the facts. But the facts supported Chanute. About the time Wilbur was reaffirming his "five year" prediction, Alberto Santos-Dumont was in Paris, making Europe's first heavier-than-air flight. A few months later, another Frenchman, Henri Farman, had even greater success. By the end of 1908, more Europeans had successfully flown heavier than air machines. On the home front, New Yorker Glenn Curtiss, a former bicycle man like the Wrights, had been building lightweight motors for dirigibles since 1903. By 1907, he was a founding member of Alexander Graham Bell's Aerial Experiment Association. Within a year, the AEA constructed and flew several different flying machines. The group's most successful machine was designed and flown by Curtiss.

Glenn Curtiss did not set out to compete with the Wrights. On several occasions, he tried to sell—then give—the Wrights one of his motors. When he first became involved with flying machines, he saw himself as the engine man and was content to let others worry about the rest of the design. As time went on, he couldn't resist the opportunity to maximize speed and power by designing and flying the machines himself. Curtiss airplanes began outperforming the Wrights' almost immediately. They were faster, capable of shorter take-offs and softer landings, and were more stable in the air. In May 1909, Curtiss incorporated America's first airplane company. (The Wrights built airplanes for sale before Curtiss but didn't incorporate their company until November of the same year.)

Chapter Fifty One

Back to Kitty Hawk, 1908

Wilbur and Orville Wright signed a contract with the U.S. Signal Corps to deliver an airplane capable of flying 40 mph, carrying two men, and traveling at least 10 miles, in February 1908. They had to deliver the plane to Fort Myer, Virginia, within 200 days for testing.

At this time, the Wrights hadn't flown since October 1905. Although they had constructed several planes at their shop in Dayton and had them ready to deliver in case suitable buyers materialized, they had never carried a passenger and never traveled 40 mph for any sustained period of time (the average, peak performance of the 1904 engine—also used in the 1905 Flyer—was 35 mph).

Still concerned about secrecy and unable to fly at Huffman Prairie without attracting unwanted attention, the Wrights decided to return to the Outer Banks that spring and prepare for their exhibition at Fort Myer. On

Remodeled 1905 Wright Flyer
at Kitty Hawk in 1908

April 4, they shipped the 1905 Flyer to Kitty Hawk. Wilbur left Dayton the next day.

The old camp at Kill Devil Hill was a mess. "Found things pretty wrecked. The side walls of the old building still stand but the roof and the north end are gone. The new building is down and torn to pieces. The pump is gone," Wilbur wrote in his diary. Men at the Kill Devil Hills Life-Saving Station told him that weather was responsible for some of the damage, vandals for the other. The missing pump was at the station but too rusted to be of any value.

While the camp was rebuilt, Wilbur stayed with the Midgetts in Kitty Hawk village and at the lifesaving station. On April 9, he hired a local

man, Oliver O'Neal, to help with construction. They started work on the
buildings on the 13th. Charles Furnas, a mechanic employed by the
Wrights, arrived at Kitty Hawk on the 15th. By the time Orville arrived
ten days later—the same day the Flyer showed up—the new building was
habitable. It took another week to get it finished and turn their attention
to the flying machine.

The Wrights began reassembling the 1905 Flyer on Monday, April
27. They made modifications to the machine as they worked, reducing the
"blinkers" on the front elevator to one and adding new, long handled control levers that required the operator to sit up while flying. Up until this
time, all flights in Wright aircraft had been made with the operator lying
down. "The sitting position for the operators will probably be more comfortable but will require regular practice before we can tackle high
winds," Wilbur recorded in his diary on May 2.

On May 4 they began testing the 1905 engine which had been
reworked in Dayton. The biggest change to the engine, said Wilbur, was
in its oiling to reduce friction and prevent overheating—an ongoing problem when flights began stretching to 20 minutes or more.

Wilbur made the first flight that either brother had made in two-and-
a-half years on May 6. He flew about one-third of a mile at 41 mph,
reaching an altitude of nearly 60 feet. Over the next week, the brothers
flew 22 times, carrying a passenger—Charlie Furnas—for the first time
on May 14.

On May 1, The *Virginian-Pilot* had published what Arthur Renstrom,
editor of the *Wright Chronology,* called "an exaggerated story." The
Wrights flew 10 miles out to sea, said the *Pilot*, and performed all sorts
of fancy maneuvers over the beach. If other interested newspapers didn't
know the Wrights were flying at Kitty Hawk again, they did now.

While the two Ohioans were hardly household names, they had
attracted national attention. Newspaper reporters had five years since the
first flights to discover the Outer Banks and how to get there. By May
12, the Tranquil House in Manteo was hosting reporters and photographers from the *New York Herald* and *American, Collier's Weekly*, the
London Daily Mail and possibly other publications.

According to biographer Fred Howard, several times that week, "the little band of journalists waded ashore from a hired launch" and was guided "through the woods of live oak, holly, and loblolly pine along the marshy shores of the Outer Banks to a place of concealment from which they could observe the Wright camp through field glasses." One reporter later complained that "with the heat, ticks, sand fleas, chiggers and mosquitos," the 4-mile trip from shore to their lookout seemed like 35.

What the reporters saw and the reports they filed left no doubt that Wilbur and Orville could fly. Finally, the fame and fortune that had eluded the Wrights for so long was to be theirs. Wilbur left Kitty Hawk for France, where, for the first time, one of the brothers would fly for the public. Orville went back to Dayton to prepare for his own debut at Fort Myer.

But by this time, others were flying in public. Others had already captured the crowd with their magic machines, however poorly they performed. They flew, that was the thing, and others got the credit for doing it. The Wrights "lost something intangible by not making the first public flights," says Crouch. They eventually received the adulation, respect and money they sought, but the passage of so much time tainted their success.

Chapter Fifty Two

Out in the open

When the Wrights made their first sales call on Europe in 1907, they went empty-handed. Their airplane, their best sales tool, was under wraps at home in Dayton. It's not surprising that they did not sell a single airplane. But they aroused a good deal of interest and realized that their best hope of making a sale was to show the world what they could do. Their patents were in place and they believed no one else could fly without using the technology they protected. And so, in 1908, after brushing up on his flying skills at Kitty Hawk, Wilbur headed to France to wow the world.

By the time Wilbur flew in France in August 1908, European aviators had already captured the headlines of the international press. Henri Farman had won the Deutsch-Archdeacon Prize for a closed-circuit flight of one kilometer earlier in the year. His countrymen Robert Esnault-Pelterie, Gabriel Voisin and Louis Bleroit were all poised to make aviation history. That Wilbur was able to capture the public's admiration and, indeed, impress just about anyone who watched him fly is a testament to how far ahead of the European competition he was.

Esnault-Pelterie was born in Switzerland but served in the French military. He was 26 years old when he flew his first powered plane in October 1907. He had begun experimenting with gliders a few years earlier, using secondhand plans for the Wright glider of 1902. Although he claimed to have duplicated the glider "exactly"—and, at first glance, it looked like the Wright glider—it was missing several key engineering details.

The performance of his "Wright" glider didn't live up to what the Wrights claimed. This discrepancy lent credence to reports circulating in Europe that the Wrights were frauds. Esnault-Pelterie reworked his Wright glider, adding his own control devices, but this improved version flew no better than his first. He also tried the first reported launch of a glider towed by an automobile. This was unsuccessful but it may have given him a taste for speed for soon he switched to designing powered airplanes.

Esnault-Pelterie is credited with inventing the first aileron (moveable pieces or flaps on an airplane wing that control roll, the rotation of an airplane on a horizontal axis from tip to tail.) He also invented the joystick-style aircraft control. Both inventions were the basis of controls still used in aircraft today.

Although wood was the material of choice at this time, Esnault-Pelterie built his airplane of steel. Its wingspan was 31.5 feet while the body measured 22.5 feet from tip to tail. It weighed nearly 800 pounds and was powered by a 30 hp, air-cooled, seven-cylinder engine.

The pilot sat in an enclosed fuselage behind the engine which drove a single propeller placed before the wings. The Wrights' airplanes, at this point, had two propellers located behind the wings and the pilot sat in an open framework next to the engine.

There's no question that Esnault-Pelterie's plane looked more sophisticated than the Wrights, but its performance was not nearly as good. One observer at the time wrote that Esnault-Pelterie's plane "could stagger into the air for brief stints." Feeble performance didn't deter the press. They reported everything.

In the meantime, the English were conducting secret trials in the Scottish highlands on a plane designed by Lt. John Dunne. Dunne, an Irishman who had been experimenting with gliders for many years on his own, had been transferred from the Royal Wiltshire Regiment to the "Balloon Factory," Britain's aeronautical research facility. (Dunne, according to Alfred Gollin in *No Longer an Island,* was the inspiration for several aviators in H.G. Wells' science fiction novels.)

Dunne's plane wouldn't fly at all, but that didn't dampen British enthusiasm. Great Britain kept its finger in the aviation pie through the promotional efforts of Lord Northcliffe, an influential London publisher. In 1908, Northcliffe established a $5,000 prize for the first flyer to cross the English Channel. Marvin McFarland, editor of *The Papers of Orville and Wilbur Wright,* claimed the prize was meant for Wilbur because Northcliffe liked the brothers and wanted to help establish their reputation. He "went so far as to offer Wilbur privately a handsome bonus if he would fly the Channel first," reported McFarland.

Although Wilbur had been flying in France for several weeks, the Channel flight was the one single, crowd-pleasing event that might have cemented his reputation as an innovative flier. He chose not to participate. Even so, Wilbur "dominated the skies that fall," wrote Crouch. "Most of his records for distance and duration stood until the following year. "Princes and millionaires" seemed to be "as thick as fleas," Wilbur reported to Orville. A "Who's Who" of European society showed up at every airfield where Wilbur flew. The Wright Flyer was "the most wonderful flying-machine that has ever been made. . . . ," reported the London *Daily Mirror.* "No such perfect control over a flying-machine has ever been known as that exercised by Mr. Wilbur Wright, the young American aeronaut, over the aeroplane in which he has for the past few days been accomplishing some marvelous flights."

But Orville, recuperating from an accident at Fort Myer, asked Wilbur not to compete in the Channel competition. "Orville's accident led the Wrights to make what in my opinion was another error of judgment, which as the result of sentimentality and perhaps even of arrogance. By all odds, Wilbur should have flown the Channel and not have left the honor to Bleroit," McFarland wrote in *Heirs to Prometheus.* "The timetable of aviation, favoring the Wrights, was irretrievably overturned."

McFarland's judgement may be too harsh. The brothers were extremely close and worried about each other's safety. Orville's request and Wilbur's agreement to skip the Channel competition may have been influenced by their belief that they had nothing to prove. But the final decision undoubtedly lay in their mutual respect and concern for the unknown dangers of flying over water.

Chapter Fifty Three

Fort Myer

On August 19, 1908, Orville left Dayton for Washington, D.C. Over the next two weeks, the reworked 1905 Flyer, flown earlier that year at Kitty Hawk, was unpacked and reassembled. Between September 3 and 17, he flew 14 times. Several flights established new records including altitude (300 feet), his personal best for duration (over one hour and 14 minutes), the longest flight with a passenger (over 9 minutes) and the first nighttime flight. The flights were witnessed by the Secretary of War, Secretary of Commerce and other government officials.

On September 17, Orville took off with Lt. Thomas Selfridge, a 26-year-old West Point graduate and the Army's expert on lighter-than-air craft. A cohort of Glenn Curtiss in the Aerial Experiment Association, he was, in fact, one of the few men in America who

Front close-up of the Wright Flyer, 1908
Lib. of Cong., Prints & Photos Div. LC-DIG-pprs-00691v

had already flown in a powered airplane. After just a few minutes in the air and at an altitude of 100 feet, Orville heard an odd tapping noise and began to prepare for landing. Before he could land, the plane lurched out of control and crashed from a height of about 75 feet. "About twenty-five feet from the ground," wrote Kelly in *The Wright Brothers*, "the machine began to right itself, and if there had been another twenty feet to go, or possibly even ten feet, it might have landed safely." But the plane dug into the ground, fatally injuring Selfridge. Orville broke his left leg, his hip and four ribs.

The crash was caused by a broken propeller. The previous week "a split had been noted in one of the original propellers," reported Crouch. Orville and Charlie Taylor had repaired it but requested a new pair of longer blades from Lorin in Dayton. These had just been installed on the plane the previous day.

After Wilbur heard of the accident in France, he wrote to Katharine, blaming himself for the mishap. "If I had been there, it would not have happened," he said. "It was not right to leave Orville to undertake such a task alone. I do not mean that Orville was incompetent to do the work itself, but I realized that he would be surrounded by thousands of people who . . . consume his time, exhaust his strength, and keep him from having proper rest. When a man is in this condition he tends to trust more to the carefulness of others instead of doing everything and examining everything himself." (Later, the brothers ran tests on a replica of the failed propeller and determined that the fault lay in its design not careless assembly.)

Had such an event taken place today, it's hard to imagine the response of the public, the news media, or the Army being as kind as it was to Orville. Other than Wilbur's private comments, there were no accusations of carelessness, no official investigation to place blame for Selfridge's death, no wrongful death lawsuit and the Army, completely satisfied with the Flyer's performance up until the time of the crash, agreed to postpone the remaining test flights to allow Orville to heal and build a new airplane.

Chapter Fifty Four

Fame, fortune and falling behind

Orville was hospitalized at Fort Myer until the end of October. Katharine Wright took a leave of absence from her teaching position in Dayton and went to Washington D.C. to help her brother. While Orville recuperated, Wilbur flew dozens of exhibitions, primarily at LeMans and Pau, France, won numerous cash prizes and started the first flying school. "Well! Hurry up and get well and get another machine ready so we can finish the American business when I get home," wrote Wilbur in early October from LeMans.

By late November, Wilbur realized that he would probably not be going home anytime soon. He needed to finish training pilots in France and had recently received an offer from Italy to fly and train pilots there. Negotiations were underway with the Russians. "I wish you could all make up your minds to come over here for a while," he wrote to Milton. In December, he wrote to Katharine: "[Pau] would be a good place for you to spend a few months. . . .We will be needing a social manager." By the end of the year, Orville and Katharine had agreed to make the trip. Milton, at age 80, decided to stay home.

The two joined Wilbur in Paris on January 12, 1909. They "were the first great celebrities of the new century," said Crouch. Wilbur, Orville, and Katharine stayed in Europe until May 5, 1909. During those five months, Wilbur's flights continued to attract the attention of European royalty and high society. The Wrights were wined and dined from London to Rome. In April Katharine was the first woman to attend a meeting of the *Aéro-Club de France*. Some of Wilbur's flights were filmed and shown on newsreels in American theaters. In March, the Wrights signed a contract with the Short Brothers in England for six airplanes. In May, negotiations for a manufacturing and sales contract were begun with a German company to open markets in Germany, Denmark, Sweden, Norway, Luxemburg and Turkey. Finally, they were being paid handsomely for their expertise.

When the Wrights arrived in New York aboard the *Kronprinzessun Cecilie* on May 11, they were greeted by huge crowds. In Dayton, two days later, a hometown crowd cheered as they were carried from the train station in a carriage drawn by four white horses. A huge celebration ending with fireworks was staged in their honor.

The brothers now found themselves spending a great deal of time dealing with the obligations of fame. Wilbur complained to Chanute about the time spent traveling "back and forth between Dayton and Washington to receive medals." He objected strongly to a celebration planned by the City of Dayton in their honor, "the excuse for an elaborate carnival and advertisement of the city under the guise of being an honor to us. As it was done in spite of our known wishes, we are not as appreciate as we might be," he added.

"I know that the reception of such honors becomes oppressive to modest men and they would avoid them if they could," joked Chanute in response, "but in this case you have brought the trouble upon yourselves by your completing the solution of a world-old problem. . . ."

After returning home in May, Orville and Wilbur set to work on a new airplane for the U.S. military. "The old one was so badly broken up that we will make all but the motor and transmission new," wrote Wilbur to Chanute. In June and July, Orville finished his flying trials at Fort Myer. Then, in August, Orville and Katharine traveled to Germany, where Orville completed negotiations for their German company and flew exhibitions for two months. While they were in Europe, Wilbur flew his first public exhibitions in the United States at the Hudson-Fulton Celebration in New York.

In spite of Orville's crash at Fort Myer, the last 12 months had been heady and financially successful. They had been given enough gold medals, honorary memberships and other awards to fill the wall of their modest home in Dayton. The University of Munich had conferred honorary doctor of engineering degrees on both men and the international press had deemed their every move and word newsworthy. It was the zenith of their popularity.

From here on out, the Wrights would never be quite so successful nor quite as glamorous. Competitors quickly took the airplane to higher levels of performance. "The majority of flyers deemed the Curtiss type (of airplane) the simplest of all to operate," wrote C. R. Roseberry in *Glenn Curtiss: Pioneer of Flight*. Roseberry quoted one pilot saying, "The Curtiss plane was a hot little devil. The Wright seemed slow-and-easy. The feeling we all had was that the Wright was dangerous in a dive, with all that wing-loading. And that chain drive was an awkward thing, besides."

Other men received credit for sensible modifications to the airplane that the Wrights themselves could have easily accomplished: wheeled landing gears, enclosed cockpits, better engines. Marvin McFarland in *Heirs to Prometheus* added other improvements that bypassed the inventors of the first practical airplane: "Any tally of developments left incomplete, untried, or postponed would have to include the perfection of pontoons and the development of the hydro-airplane, landing and taking off from a ship, the substitution of tractor for pusher propulsion, the abandonment of the clever but cumbersome bicycle-chain drive. . . ."

Lawsuits over the Wright patents filled the next few years and, later, acrimonious dealings with the Smithsonian Institution over placement of the 1903 Wright Flyer tarnished their image. Wilbur's demand that the use of his name be dropped from the Broadway play "Inconstant George" in late 1909 and other public pettiness added to their image in professional circles as difficult people.

Chapter Fifty Five

1910 -1911

Exterior side view of the Wright Co. factory Dayton, Ohio
Lib. of Cong., Prints & Photos Div. LC-DIG-pprs-00687v

By the beginning of 1910, the Wrights were immersed in the business of airplanes. It was ironic, wrote Peter Jakab in *Visions of Flying Machines*, that "just as the Wrights began to reap the full fruit of their years of labor, the rest of the aeronautical world was passing them by. . . . The brothers never carried the development of their invention beyond the 1905 airplane in any meaningful way." But, he went on to say, it was unfair to expect more from them: "They had done enough." If the Wrights noticed they were being left behind, they did not comment on the fact.

In January, ground was broken for the first Wright Co. factory in Dayton. By the end of the year, it was producing two airplanes a month. The company introduced a new airplane design, the Model B, in late June. A month later it was modified to include wheels. It was the first time wheels were used on a Wright plane, although they were already standard equipment on other planes. Another new Wright plane, the Model R, dubbed the "Baby Grand" was introduced in October. Although it attained speeds of up to 80 mph it was still outperformed by other aircraft. In November, a Wright airplane carried ten bolts of fabric for the Morehouse-Martens Co. from Dayton to Columbus. It was the first known flight to carry commercial freight in the United States or abroad.

The Wrights resisted getting into the exhibition business although as early as 1907 they had made inquiries to Barnum & Bailey about managing such a program if and when they decided to do it. Finally, after Curtiss and others had been flying for the public for more than a year, the Wrights formed the Wright Exhibition Co. in March 1910 and named Roy Knabenshue as its manager. Orville trained five exhibition flyers in Montgomery, Alabama, that spring. Later in the year, The Wright Co. opened a pilot training school at Huffman Prairie. Orville, once again, was in charge of instruction.

May was the month for several milestones in the Wrights' personal flying history: Wilbur and Orville flew together for the first and only time (Orville piloted), and Orville took Milton, now 82 years old, for his first airplane ride.

Even though they now shared the aeronautical limelight with others, Wilbur and Orville were still in demand at aviation events and at social functions honoring the growing aeronautical industry. Neither man liked public appearances but both attended when necessary and Wilbur on occasion would speak a few words. They attended several functions throughout the year, from air shows to banquets and college graduation ceremonies.

Octave Chanute died on November 23 and Wilbur attended his funeral although their friendship had been damaged that year in an argument over their wing-warping patent. Wilbur wrote a tribute to Chanute, published shortly after Chanute's death. It summed up Chanute's contribution to the Wrights' success although Wilbur's only personal comment was to say that Chanute had "encouraged" the Wrights "to persevere in their experiments."

"(Chanute's) labors had vast influence in bringing about the era of human flight," Wilbur wrote. "His writings were so lucid as to provide an intelligent understanding of the nature of the problems of flight to a vast number of persons who would probably never have given the matter study otherwise, and not only by published articles, but by personal correspondence and visitation, he inspired and encouraged to the limits of his ability all who were devoted to the work. . . . No one was too humble to receive a share of his time."

The year 1911 was little different from 1910. Business, not flying, occupied both brothers. With a staff of exhibition pilots, neither had many

Orville working on his glider at Kill Devil Hill, 1911
Photo courtesy Outer Banks History Center

occasions to fly. Wilbur flew an airplane in public for the last time in April while training pilots in Germany although, curiously, he did most of his training on the ground. It appears that he only took to the air to prove a point to a recalcitrant German captain: "He would not believe that I could carry two men at 375 turns of the propellers till I took him up and did it," Wilbur wrote to Orville.

Fred Kelly in *Miracle at Kitty Hawk* claimed that "Wilbur, after his first few flights, would just as soon have stayed on the ground; he flew only for business." The gist of Kelly's observation may have been correct, but his timing was wrong. Wilbur clearly relished his flying time in Europe in 1908 and 1909. Perhaps, after hundreds of flights, he became bored with the activity. Orville, on the other hand, said Kelly, "continued to enjoy flying for the sport of the thing," even after his crash at Fort Myer. In any case, Wilbur—who in 1911 had a full plate of patent litigation—stopped flying.

Orville flight-tested a new hydroplane built for the U.S. Navy in July. In late August, he participated in training flights for the U.S. Signal Corps at Simms Station. In October, he decided to go to Kitty Hawk to conduct gliding experiments again. His brother Lorin and Lorin's son Horace went along. Alexander Ogilvie, a friend

Orville and his helpers carrying a glider across the sand at Kill Devil Hill, 1911
Photo courtesy Outer Banks History Center

from England, also made the trip. Orville stayed for three weeks, making about 90 glides from Kill Devil Hill and nearby dunes. Although he crashed twice without injury, he also established a new soaring record of 9 minutes, 45 seconds, that wasn't broken for 10 years.

In November, the Wrights disbanded their exhibition team. The exhibition business had lived up to the Wrights' worst fears. "I want no stunts and spectacular frills put on the flights," Wilbur warned his pilots. "Anything beyond plain flying will be chalked up as a fault and not as a credit." But the competition between exhibition flyers was keen and such warnings went unheeded. Early that month, Ralph Johnstone, one of the team's original pilots had crashed at a show and died. He was the first American pilot to die in a plane crash. (Over the next six months, five more of the Wright's original exhibition team would die in crashes of Wright airplanes.)

In November, both brothers flew a Curtiss machine at Huffman Prairie "to gain familiarity with the control mechanisms which they claimed infringed the Wright patents," reported Arthur Renstrom in the *Wright Chronology*. It was Wilbur's last flight.

Chapter Fifty Six

The patent wars

The Wrights began filing patent infringement lawsuits in August 1909. Wilbur, who had gained extensive legal experience helping his father with lawsuits involving the Church of the United Brethren, took primary responsibility for stopping the unauthorized (and free) use of wing-warping, something they believed to be their patented invention. It consumed most of his attention and energy until his death in May 1912 at the age of 45.

Orville was also involved, providing technical information for Wilbur and giving depositions. After Wilbur's death, he continued to fight the legal battles started by his brother—and began a few new ones of his own.

As far as the Wrights were concerned, no one could fly without wing-warping and, therefore, anyone who built a successful airplane owed them a licensing fee. Not only did the Wrights attempt to enforce their patents by suing the manufacturers of airplanes, they took legal action against anyone making money from the flying of those planes. When the Wrights were attacked in the press for these actions, reported Renstrom, they defended themselves saying the patent laws of the United States were too lax.

In less than four years, the Wrights filed suits against Herring-Curtiss Co., Glenn Curtiss, the Aeronautic Society of New York; Ralph Saulnier, Claude Grahame-White and Louis Paulhan (for importing a French airplane to the United States that the Wrights claimed infringed on their patents); Aero Corporation, Ltd.; Henri Farman, Louis Bléroit and others in France; René Barrier, René Simon and St. Croix Johnstone; and the promoters of the Chicago International Aviation Meet.

Their right to profit through licensing agreements that acknowledged their patents seemed clear-cut to the Wrights. Their competitors and the courts were never completely convinced, however, that the Wrights' claims were just. Although initial court rulings favored the Wrights' claim, in retrospect, most experts believe the rulings were wrong in both legal and technical applications. Curtiss, in particular, was considered by most of his peers and the aeronautical community to be innocent of patent infringement but guilty of hiring inept lawyers.

Although Orville eventually settled his differences with Curtiss and went into business with him, he "blamed Curtiss in some measure for Wilbur's loss," wrote Roseberry in his biography of Curtiss. He quoted Orville saying that the death must be charged "to our long struggle. . . . The delays (in the Curtiss lawsuit) were what worried him to death."

In addition to lawsuits they initiated, the Wrights had to deal with lawsuits in which they were the defendants. In 1910, the Wrights were sued by Erastus E. Winkley, who claimed he had suggested an automatic control he invented for sewing machines could be used in airplanes prior to the Wrights' patent. Two years later, Charles Lamson sued the Wrights for infringement of his kite patent. It's possible both of these men believed they had a legitimate claim. More likely, they hoped to profit from an out-of-court settlement or a judicial error. Both were found in the Wrights' favor but they were tiresome all the same.

During this same time, Orville and Wilbur were trying to secure their patents. Even with patent attorneys to file the paperwork, the applications required the Wrights' personal involvement. When the German Patent Office invalidated several basic features of their German patents, the brothers became personally involved in the appeal process.

For three years after Wilbur's death, court appearances and depositions occupied much of Orville's time. In 1915, Orville sold the Wright Co. and left the patent suits to its new owners. The suits and their subsequent appeals came to an end when, during World War I, American airplane manufacturers signed a cross-licensing agreement.

Chapter Fifty Seven

Orville on his own

Orville and Katharine (who never returned to her teaching job after Orville's accident at Fort Myer) spent a month in Europe in early 1913. It was their last trip abroad. Back at home, Orville continued to work on his hydroplane (Curtiss had already built a practical model) and on an automatic stabilizer. He traveled extensively to meetings, court hearings, air shows and honorary events. Katharine frequently accompanied him.

According to Crouch, Orville began buying up Wright Co. stock in 1914. His goal was to gain control and sell the company, ridding himself of the management obligations he inherited when Wilbur died. After the sale was completed in 1915, he stayed on the payroll as a consulting engineer until the company merged with two other companies in 1916. When that agreement ended, he started the Wright Aeronautical Laboratory in Dayton and for two years worked as an aeronautical consultant to the U.S. government and private companies. In 1917, after the Wright Co. closed its Dayton plant, Orville became consulting engineer for the Dayton Airplane Co. Within a few months Dayton Airplane reorganized as the Dayton-Wright Airplane Co. Orville served as a director and consulting engineer although his directorship was purely as a figurehead. He owned no stock in either company.

The same month the new company was incorporated, Orville was commissioned a major in the aviation section of the Signal Officers Reserve Corps. He served at home, working with the engineers at Dayton-Wright to fulfill government contracts for more than 4,000 airplanes. His success was limited. The first 400 planes the company delivered were late and defective. The remainder of the order was never completed, wrote Fred Howard, and the few planes that made their way to Europe before the war ended were considered "flaming coffins."

General Motors bought the company in 1919 and closed its doors in 1923. Orville continued in his role as consulting engineer and during this time, working with another engineer, James Jacobs, developed and patented the split-flap. "Like Orville's automatic stabilizer of 1913," wrote Howard, "the split-flap airfoil was brought to a state of usefulness by another inventor."

Orville's only new invention that earned any money after 1917 was a mechanical toy granted a patent in 1925. The toy was manufactured by a Dayton company headed by Orville's brother Lorin.

In May 1918, Orville piloted an airplane—a 1911 Wright biplane—for the last time. From 1918 on, Orville puttered in his laboratory and at his Dayton home. He vacationed for three months each summer on a private island in Ontario, Canada, evidently quite happy with the isolation. The rest of each year brought dozens of invitations to aeronautical conferences, social events, fundraisers, award ceremonies and other gatherings where his presence might serve some purpose—almost all of which he would have rather not attended.

Orville corresponded with hundreds of people seeking his advice on aeronautical matters or his support for some aeronautical venture. "[He] received hundreds of letters from aspiring or disgruntled inventors, most of which he answered, often at great cost of time, effort, and even of research," wrote Marvin McFarland, editor of *The Papers of Wilbur and Orville Wright*.

In 1925, a sore relationship between the Wrights and the Smithsonian Institution got sorer when Orville decided to donate the 1903 Flyer to the Science Museum in London, England. Problems with the Smithsonian began in 1910 when its Secretary made the decision to not accept the 1903 plane for exhibit and, instead, asked for a model of the plane Orville flew at Fort Myer. At the time, a model of Langley's Aerodrome was on display and identified as having flown. The information appeared to the Wrights to be an attempt to give more credit to Langley than was his due. The model did fly, but the full-sized plane did not. To make matters worse, as part of the display, a plaque was hung giving credit to Langley for discoveries that belonged to Lilienthal. Whether the Smithsonian was deliberately distorting the truth or was greatly uninformed was never determined because the Wrights, as they typically did when confronted with what they assumed to be malevolence, simply ignored the

Smithsonian's correspondence.

That wasn't Orville's only grievance. In 1913 the Smithsonian had awarded the Langley Medal to Glenn Curtiss who had recently been found guilty of infringing upon the Wrights' patents. A year later, Curtiss asked the Smithsonian for permission to attempt to fly Langley's Aerodrome. He was given permission to take the machine to his Hammondsport, New York shop where he made modifications based on "knowledge of aerodynamics discovered by the Wrights but never possessed by Langley," claimed Kelly, the Wrights' biographer. After Curtiss made "several short hops, of less than five seconds," the Smithsonian reported that Langley's plane had flown. The report failed to note that the plane had been modified. After Curtiss's "flights," the machine was restored to its original condition, reinstalled at the Smithsonian and identified as the "first man-carrying aeroplane in the history of the world capable of sustained free flight."

It appears likely that Charles Walcott, Secretary of the Smithsonian at the time, was behind these efforts to discredit the Wrights. In 1916, Alexander Graham Bell tried to intercede on the Wrights' behalf. At Bell's insistence, Walcott wrote to the Wrights suggesting there might be a place for the 1903 plane. But in a face-to-face meeting, "Orville found that Walcott's attitude had not changed. . . . ," reported Kelly.

Before completing his gift of the 1903 plane to the London museum, Orville attempted to resolve his dispute with the Smithsonian. After three more years and more rebuffs by Walcott, he gave up and shipped the plane overseas. Walcott died in 1927 and his successor, Charles Abbott, attempted to patch things up with Orville. But it wasn't until 1942, when Abbott finally made the public statement acknowledging the Smithsonian's error that an agreement to bring the plane back to America was reached. The plane was unveiled in the North Hall of the Smithsonian's Arts and Industries building on December 17, 1948, eleven months after Orville died.

The Outer Banks Remembers

The Wright Brothers National Monument at Kill Devil Hill
Photo by Gus Martin, courtesy Outer Banks History Center

Chapter Fifty Eight

Life goes on

William James Tate
Photo courtesy Grady Tate

Of all the Outer Banks residents who had contact with the Wright brothers, only William Tate left any substantial record of what their impact was on his life. "Bill Tate was the one person who got into what the Wrights were doing and kept up with it," said Bill Harris, a Kitty Hawk native whose family lived on the banks when the Wright brothers visited the area. "He may have been the only one who realized what the Wrights were actually doing. . . . If anybody kept the Wright brothers legend alive in Kitty Hawk, it was Bill Tate."

Over the years, Tate was called upon to provide details of the Wrights and the time they spent at Kitty Hawk—and he was happy to oblige. Known in the village as a talker and self-promoter, he spent years in local politics and in a long string of civil service jobs that afforded him the opportunity to keep abreast of opportunities to tell his stories. For the 25th and 40th anniversaries of the first flights, Tate published his recollections; both articles were included in *The Published Writings of Wilbur and Orville Wright*, edited by Peter Jakab and Rick Young. "They merit inclusion . . . because of the unique perspective they bring," wrote the editors. "Tate, a witness to and a participant in the Wrights' glider trials, was a historical player in critical aspects of the Wright story." He was not the most accurate historian—dates and details changed from one telling to another—but he was the only contemporary of the Wrights at Kitty Hawk who wrote about this piece of village history.

Much to his dismay, Tate did not witness the first flights on December 17, 1903. He had moved from the village to Martin's Point before the Wrights returned to the Outer Banks in 1903, making the trip to the Kill Devil Hill camp an all-day excursion. Although Wilbur had invited him to come watch, Tate believed the weather too bad for flying. Some accounts said he stayed at home, some said he traveled to Elizabeth City on business. The confusion probably arose from Tate's own telling of the tale.

Because of his association with the Wrights and subsequent interest in aviation, Tate joined the National Aeronautical Association and played a role in planning the monuments erected on the Outer Banks to honor the Wrights. According to Tate, he first proposed a memorial to the brothers in 1912 after Wilbur's death in a letter written to the Custodian of the Hall of History in Raleigh although no action was taken on this suggestion. When Congressman Lindsay Warren took up the cause of a national monument at Kill Devil Hill several years later, Tate wrote letters of support for the project.

In 1928, Tate was instrumental in getting a marker placed in front for his old home in Kitty Hawk village where the Wrights stayed when they first arrived on the Outer Banks. Tate was still living in that house during their subsequent visits in 1901 and 1902. In 1915, he moved from Martin's Point to the Currituck mainland where he served as keeper of the Long Point light at Coinjock. He died in 1953, six months short of the fiftieth anniversary of the first flight.

According to Thomas Parramore, in *Triumph at Kitty Hawk*, Tate was the head of the North Carolina branch of the NAA

Dan Tate
Photo courtesy Grady Tate

in 1932 and "threw his efforts into a campaign to force the Smithsonian to recognize the Wrights' achievement and to persuade Orville to allow the plane to come home."

Bill Tate's half-brother, Dan, had parted company with the Wrights in

1903 before their historic flight in a disagreement over collecting fire-wood. Although the Wrights had recently agreed to his demand for a pay raise (he was now paid $7 weekly when most day workers on the Outer Banks earned only $3.50 to $4.50), he was displeased with the work he was asked to do. Orville called him "spoiled" in a letter to Katharine. Bill Tate apologized for his brother in a letter to Wilbur: "Dan played the fool & left you. He evidently does not know what is best for him." Dan died in 1905. He is pictured in several surviving photographs, helping the Wrights fly their gliders as kites and launching their manned gliders.

Tom Tate and his wife on their wedding day
Photo courtesy Grady Tate

Dan's young son Tom was loaded onto the 1900 glider and flown as if on a kite. Tom was immortalized in a photograph snapped by one of the brothers holding a drum fish "almost as large as he," wrote Orville in another letter home. "Tom is a small chap . . . that can tell more big yarns than any kid of his size I ever saw."

Another of Dan's sons, Sam, was about five years old when the Wright brothers first came to Kitty Hawk. In later years, he passed on what stories he knew about the Wrights to his family. One that he particularly enjoyed retelling, said his daughter-in-law, Suzanne, was about the time his father took him to the Wrights' camp around breakfast time. The Wrights' love of eggs was legendary among the village folk. Not only did the Ohio boys buy up as much of the local production as they could, they kept a hen at their Kill Devil Hill camp to supplement their supply. Dan and Sam were invited to join the Wrights for their meal as extra eggs were added to the skillet. "Those eggs were so good," Sam would tell his family, maybe the best eggs he'd ever eaten.

Two of Bill Tate's children took up their father's interest in flight. Irene, who turned three the first year the Wrights visited Kitty Hawk and wore dresses made from the wing fabric of their first glider, married a professional aviator and took up flying herself. Bill's son Elijah, born in 1902, worked as a mechanic for Glenn Curtiss.

Years later, Elijah Baum, the boy who met Wilbur Wright on the beach when he first arrived in Kitty Hawk, told interviewers that he missed the flight because he "didn't think it was worth the walk from Kitty Hawk." Even in retrospect, he didn't regret his decision, said Parramore. "A sense of awe, an immediate recognition that men had performed what many thought could never be done, is distinctly lacking in the witnesses' reflections."

Harris's family had little to say about the famous brothers. His relatives hauled freight for the Wrights and in 1903 shipped the Wright Flyer back to Dayton. Even so, he didn't grow up hearing stories about the Wrights. When Harris began collecting oral histories from older villagers for a college project, he expected to uncover a treasure trove of memories. For the most part, he learned very little. "The community really did not pay that much attention to them," Harris said.

Mary Midgett, the wife of Capt. Franklin Midgett, was one of the few villagers who recalled more than "they were nice, gentlemanly and well-dressed." She recalled that both Wilbur and Orville had spent the night with her family in Kitty Hawk. (Beginning in 1902, the brothers used Midgett's *Lou Willis* for transportation. When the captain arrived at the village late at night or needed to leave at daybreak, they would spend the night at his home, explained Harris.) Mary recalled that Orville "done more talking. He was full of talking while Wilbur set around like he was studying." For some reason, Lorin Wright, who visited Kitty Hawk in 1902 and 1911, made a bigger impression on Mary than his brothers. When Harris asked her what she thought about the Wrights trying to fly, she said, "I never had no thought about it, and I didn't know what other people thought."

Truxton Midgett, Mary's son, was a teenager when the Wrights first came to Kitty Hawk. Truxton's family lived near the Tates. He also recalled Lorin and mentioned George Spratt who was at the Wright camp in 1901, 1902 and 1903. He told Harris that he had helped crate and ship the Wright Flyer used at Kitty Hawk in 1908. It wasn't heavy, he said, "but it was too long for local boats." When Harris asked if he'd kept any pieces of the plane as a souvenir, Truxton replied, "a piece wouldn't have been more valuable than any old hickory stick then, although now lots of people claim to have pieces."

The Wrights were "pretty straight" and liked their privacy, he recalled. "They didn't do any visiting."

If the Ohioans did visit with other villagers, all the parties involved must have kept it to themselves. "From what I can tell, they only associated with the Tates and Dr. Cogswell (who was married to Addie Tate's sister and lived nearby)," said Harris. But the Wrights' diaries make note of visits to the local lifesaving stations, to Capt. James Hobbs and his wife, Eliza, and to many occasions when locals came by to visit and were invited to stay for dinner. "Rev. Mr. Davis, pastor of Kitty Hawk M.E. Church, called on us and took dinner with us," wrote Orville in his diary on October 22, 1903. Three days later, "Mr. John Moss of Colington Island stopped with us several hours and stayed for dinner." A couple weeks later, Reverend Davis was back bringing a "Mr. Hallowell" who invited the Wrights to a theatrical performance in Kitty Hawk. In spite of Rev. Davis's visits, no one remembers either Wright ever attending church in the village.

Alpheus Drinkwater was another Outer Banks resident whose life intersected with the Wrights. He was working as a telegraph operator at the Currituck Beach weather station north of Kitty Hawk during their 1903 visit. Most historians believe he was invited to watch the December 17 flights but chose not to come because he was covering news of the *Moccasin,* a Navy submarine that became stranded near his station. Drinkwater, a popular local figure, later claimed to have been the operator who sent the Wrights' telegram announcing their success. He was mistaken: Joe Dosher at Kitty Hawk was given the telegram directly by the Wrights who were present when he relayed it to Norfolk. (Drinkwater was working as a telegraph operator in Manteo when the Wrights returned to the Outer Banks in 1908, however, and did send several telegrams about their flights during that trip. Some historians have suggested Drinkwater simply confused the two events.) It appears that locals didn't question Drinkwater's claim, made years after the fact and in spite of conflicting eyewitness accounts. During his lifetime and for years after, Drinkwater enjoyed celebrity as the local messenger who transmitted the news of the first flight to the world.

Chapter Fifty Nine

Building a monument . . . or two

According to biographer Tom Crouch, the first American monument honoring the Wrights was erected in 1927 in Bill Tate's former Kitty Hawk yard where Wilbur may have assembled the 1900 glider. Villagers raised over $200 to build this 5-foot marble obelisk that still stands today well off the beaten path. The Tates' home, however, is long gone, destroyed by fire in 1928.

The idea of a Wright memorial to commemorate their first flights at Kitty Hawk is credited to Lindsay Warren, a Washington, North Carolina, native elected to the U.S. House of Representatives in 1924. He believed the memorial and the traffic it would generate would force the state to build bridges and roads linking the Outer Banks to the mainland. Roads and tourism all but guaranteed a growing economy for the area

Monument marking the location of the Tate home in Kitty Hawk

Photo by Aycock Brown, courtesy Outer Banks History Center

which, at the time, lagged far behind the rest of the state. From a national perspective, the Wright brothers were symbols of America's contribution to the world. According to a National Park Service administrative history written by Andrew Hewes in 1962, the memorial was expected to express "gratitude on the part of a prospering and airplane-conscious nation." He must have had conversations in Washington that led him to believe the idea would be well-received.

Rep. Warren began work on legislation for the memorial in April 1926. He wanted to introduce the bill on December 17 of that year and request that the monument be completed in time for the 25th anniversary of the first flights. He wrote letters to Orville in August and again in November asking for his support but received no answer. Warren introduced the bill as planned, asking for an appropriation of $50,000 for a memorial to be located at Kill Devil Hill. Warren's bill was eventually shelved because Hiram Bingham, former governor of Connecticut and a noted historian, as well as president of the National Aeronautic Association, introduced a similar bill in the Senate the same day. Because a Senate bill was more prestigious than one from the House, Warren's bill was dropped. Bingham's passed both houses and was signed by President Coolidge in March 1927.

Although several historians suggest Bingham acted on Warren's behalf, a letter Warren sent to Bingham on December 17 makes it clear that was not the case. "I see that you today introduced in the Senate a bill for a memorial to the first successful air-plane flight made at Kitty Hawk . . . . It so happens that I introduced practically the same bill also today. I am very glad to know your interest, and I have quite a large file on the subject which I will be glad to place at your disposal," he wrote.

It is more likely that Bingham was acting at the urging of Herbert Hoover, Secretary of Commerce, who had his own agenda for honoring the Wrights. Hoover believed a growing aviation industry would be good for the American economy and had the potential to provide the country with faster, more efficient transportation. His objectives in 1923 were detailed by Ray Wilbur and Arthur Hyde in their 1937 study of Hoover's government service: 1. Create a national airways system similar to the national waterways; 2. Appropriate a mail subsidy to increase aviation transportation and get mail delivery out of government hands and into the private sector; 3. Create an auxiliary to defense, providing personnel and manufacturing capacity from the private sector in time of war; 4. Regulate pilots and machines to improve safety; 5. Encourage scientific research into aviation problems; and 6. Create a government agency to administer these services.

Secretary of War Dwight Davis and Secretary of the Navy Curtis Wilbur shared Hoover's interest in selling the public on the value of airplanes and a national aviation initiative. All three knew public support was a political necessity for the increased funding they each sought from Congress to accomplish their goals.

Davis, Wilbur, and Hoover were named in Bingham's bill to serve as a commission to select the location, acquire land and supervise the construction of the monument. The project was designated an historic site—officially known as the Kill Devil Hill National Memorial until 1953 when its name was changed to the Wright Brothers National Memorial—under the aegis of the War Department. (The site was transferred to the National Park Service in 1933.)

According to Hewes, Hoover made a personal inspection of the proposed memorial site shortly after the bill was approved. After the visit, Hoover is credited with suggesting that a marine beacon be used on the memorial as a tribute to the lifesaving service and the assistance its crews gave the Wrights. In what may have been a *quid pro quo* with Warren, Hoover also voiced his concern over spending taxpayer money for a monument that would be inaccessible to most of America. Warren used this to begin pressuring the state to build new roads and a bridge from Currituck to Kitty Hawk.

During the summer of 1927, the Kill Devil Hills Memorial Association was formed, according to Hewes, "to insure a proper memorialization of the Wrights and their first flight." Its real purpose may have been to support Warren's efforts to get roads built. According to W. O. Saunders, editor of the Elizabeth City *Independent* and the association's first president, the group's slogan was "Build the last link from Murphy to Manteo." Several prominent national figures were asked to serve on the association's honorary advisory council. Herbert Hoover, Charles Lindbergh, Alfred E. Smith, Joseph Pulitzer, Commander Richard Byrd, General John Pershing, William Randolph Hearst and Harry Guggenheim were among those who accepted.

The association, not the federally-appointed commission, soon arranged the donation of 200 acres for the memorial from Frank Stick, Charles Baker, Allen Heuth and the Carolina Development Co. But the several government agencies charged with approving a design for the monument argued over plans for more than a year. Nothing was decided by December 17, 1928, and so for the 25th anniversary, a symbolic first cornerstone of the monument was laid on top of the hill and a boulder was placed to mark the site where the Wrights' plane was launched at the base of the hill.

In February 1928, Rep. Warren asked Orville Wright if he would consider placing the 1903 airplane at the monument site. Wright declined. He preferred to give the plane to a larger museum to be part of an exhibit honoring the history of all aviation, he said, or to the City of Dayton. He ended up sending the plane

Ceremony on December 17, 1928, marking the 25th anniversary of the first flight
Photo courtesy Outer Banks History Center

to the Science Museum of London. In 1948, after years of negotiations—first with Orville, later with his heirs—the plane was returned to the U.S. and put on display at the Smithsonian Institution. Without a plane or any other significant artifacts to showcase, funds for a museum at the Kill Devil Hill site were not forthcoming

In 1929, with plans for the monument still up in the air, work began on stabilizing Kill Devil Hill, which was estimated to have moved at least 400 feet to the southwest since 1903. A competition was held for the monument design and a jury, under the guidance of the American Institute of Architects, selected the entry that was built. Senator Bingham, however, was unhappy with the selection. Hewes quoted Bingham saying the design was "grotesque" and "an abortion." Bingham's objections slowed down the approval process. Orville Wright was asked for his opinion on the design but he declined to comment. Twice, Warren asked President Hoover to help end the design deadlock. Hoover expressed strong interest in seeing the project completed but exactly what he did to end the deadlock is unknown. But shortly after Warren's last request, Bingham withdrew his opposition vote on the committee holding up the monument's design approval.

Finally, a construction contract was let to Wills & Mafera Corporation, New York, for $213,000. According to Hewes, "specifications called for a granite tower 61 feet in height and a base of 36 by 43 feet. . . . The tower was to include a light beacon." Nearly 1,200 tons of granite for the monument and its platform were purchased from the Sargent Granite Company

Overhead view of Wright Brothers Monument design
Photo courtesy Outer Banks History Center

of Mount Airy, North Carolina, shipped via railroad to Norfolk or Elizabeth City and then moved by truck or barge to the Outer Banks. It took a little over one year for a crew of 45 to 60 men to complete the monument.

Orville Wright and President Hoover, along with several other dignitaries, requested that William J. Tate be named caretaker of the monument. But the appointment, made at the direction of the War Department's Quartermaster General, went to Joseph Partridge, a civilian who had been employed at the site during construction.

Dedication of Wright Brothers monument, November 19, 1932
Photo from the National Archives, courtesy Outer Banks History Center

The monument was dedicated on November 19, 1932, with Orville Wright as the guest of honor. In spite of arrangements to accommodate 20,000 people—including bleachers for 2,000 and parking for 1,000 cars —a bad storm kept the crowd to around 1,000. Several members of the Wright family traveled by train from Dayton to Washington, D.C. and from there to Norfolk by steamer and then by car to Kill Devil Hills for the ceremony. Orville, as usual, made no speech but was quoted afterwards saying the monument was "distinctive without being freakish."

The Kill Devil Hills Memorial Association was reorganized in 1951 as the Kill Devil Hills Memorial Society. (This group became the First Flight Society in 1966.) National in scope, one of its priorities was to get a museum and reconstructions of the Wrights' field buildings and launch rail constructed on the memorial grounds. Additional land was acquired for the site in 1954 but nothing further happened. According to Outer Banks historian David Stick, a campaign to interest the airplane industry in funding a visitor center in 1957 also went nowhere. The current visitor center was finally approved and funded in the late 1950s. Now on the Register of National Historic Buildings, it was dedicated in December 1960.

The Outer Banks location of the memorial had always been somewhat controversial. The area was remote; many considered Dayton a better choice because of its accessibility as well as its obvious importance to the Wrights' story. But Kill Devil Hill prevailed and millions of people have found their way to it. Every year in the past decade, a half-million people—give or take a few thousand—have come to the sand flats below the hill and walked the 120 feet that Orville first flew on December 17, 1903, to the spot 852 feet out that marks Wilbur's final flight of the day. They have climbed to the top of the tall dune and looked out across sand and water as Wilbur and Orville must have done dozens of times. The view has changed in the last hundred years but the "steady winds" Bill Tate promised them still blow.

Afterword

The Wrights were very private people—maybe more secretive than most, but also typical of their times. In the Victorian era which shaped them, personal revelations were considered gauche. Men were not in touch with their inner selves; public talk of emotions was avoided; displays of enthusiasm could mark one as ill-bred. Although the Wrights left behind an enormous collection of correspondence and other written materials, little of it sheds any light on the soul and substance of either man. And news reporters of their day respected the Wrights' wishes to remain at arm's length. It would be impossible for anyone in their shoes today to escape with their starched collars intact without our knowing what brand of starch they used and who did the ironing. As it is, we know very little about their personal lives except what the Wrights themselves wanted us to know.

But, no matter how much the Wrights wanted us to stick with the facts of their invention, the story of how they made history is more than one of having the right stuff at the right time. It is also the story of two men who defied the odds and achieved their dream but never fully enjoyed the sweetness of their success. In the end, it's the Wrights' fragile humanity and obvious genius that fascinates as much as the fact that, thanks to their determination to fly, men and women can now soar with the control and daring of birds—aloft at last.

Selected Bibliography

Bates, Jo Anna Heath. Editor, *The Heritage of Currituck County North Carolina*. Winston-Salem, NC: Albemarle Genealogical Society, Inc. in cooperation with the Currituck County Historical Society and Hunter Publishing Co., 1985.

Bernstein, Mark. *Grand Eccentrics*. Wilmington, Ohio: Orange Frazer Press, 1996.

Bishir, Catherine W. *The "Unpainted Aristocracy": The Beach Cottages of Old Nags Head*. Raleigh, NC: Division of Archives and History, North Carolina Department of Cultural Resources. 1987.

Brown, Aycock. *The Birth of Aviation*. Winston-Salem, NC: The Collins Co., 1953.

Brunsman, Charlotte K. and August E. *Wright & Wright Printers*. Kettering, Ohio: Trailside Press, 1989.

Chanute, Octave. *Gliding Experiments*, Chicago: Journal of the Western Society of Engineers, Vol.2 1897.

_____ *Progress in Flying Machines*. New York: Dover Publications, 1997.

Combs, Harry with Martin Caidin. *Kill Devil Hill*. Boston: Houghton Mifflin Co., 1979.

Crouch, Tom D. *The Giant Leap*. Columbus, Ohio: The Ohio Historical Society, 1971.

_____ *A Dream of Wings*. Washington, DC: Smithsonian Institution Press, 1989.

_____ *The Bishops' Boys*. New York: W. W. Norton & Co., 1989.

Drury, Rev. A. W. *History of the City of Dayton and Montgomery County Ohio*: Chicago: S. J. Clarke Publishing Co., 1909.

Fisk, Fred C. and Marlin W. Todd. *The Wright Brothers from Bicycle to Biplane* Dayton, Ohio: Fisk & Todd, 2000.

Fleischman, John and Robert Kunzig. *Photography, Old and New Again*. Discover, Vol. 23, February 2002.

Geibert, Ronald R. and Patrick B. Nolan. *Kitty Hawk and Beyond*. Dayton, Ohio: Wright State University Press, 1990.

Gibbs-Smith, Charles H. *The Wright Brothers*. London: Her Majesty's Stationery Office, 1963.

_____ *The Rebirth of European Aviation*. London: Her Majesty's Stationery Office, 1974.

Gollin, Alfred. *No Longer an Island*. Stanford, CA: Stanford University Press, 1984.

Hallion, Richard P. *The Wright Brothers: Heirs to Prometheus*. Washington, D.C.: Smithsonian Institution Press, 1978.

Harris, Bill. Interviews with the author, 2002.

_____ *Oral History Project* (taped interviews with Kitty Hawk village residents), 1960-1979.

Harris, Sherwood. *First to Fly*. New York: Simon & Schuster, 1970.

Hewes, Andrew M. *National Park Service–The Wright Brothers National Memorial: An Administrative History*. Unpublished manuscript, 1962.

Howard, Fred. *Wilbur and Orville*. Mineola, NY: Dover Publications, 1998.

Hunt, Melba. *Cooking the Wright Way*. Kettering, Ohio: Kettering-Moraine Museum, 1998.

Jakab, Peter L. and Rick Young. *The Published Writings of Wilbur and Orville Wright*. Washington, DC: Smithsonian Institution Press, 2000.

Jakab, Peter L. *Visions of a Flying Machine*. Washington, D.C.: Smithsonian Institution Press, 1990.

John, Jeffrey Alan. *A Flying Machine, or a Patch of Sky?* VCQ, Spring 2001.

Junior League of Dayton, Ohio. Editor. *Dayton: A History in Photographs*: Dayton, Ohio. 1976.

Kelly, Fred C. *The Wright Brothers*. New York: Dover Publications, 1989.

_____ *Miracle at Kitty Hawk*. New York: DeCapo Press, 1996.

Khoury, Angel Ellis. *Manteo: A Roanoke Island Town*. Virginia Beach, VA: The Donning Co., 1999.

Kirk, Stephen. *First in Flight*. Winston-Salem, NC: John F. Blair, Publisher, 1995.

Launius, Roger D. *Innovation and the Development of Flight.* College Station, Texas: Texas A&M University Press, 1999.

Layman, R. D. *Dirigibles, Airships, Zeppelins and Blimps.* Relevance, the Quarterly Journal of the Great War Society, Winter 1996.

Lilienthal, Otto. *Birdflight as the Basis of Aviation.* Hummelstown, PA: Markowski International Publishers, 2001.

Mason, Robert. *Setting the Record Straight on the First Flight.* Southern Pines, NC: The Pilot, 1999.

_____ *When Flying Was News.* Norfolk, VA: The Virginian-Pilot, Sunday, December 17, 1950.

Maxim, Hiram. *A New Flying-Machine: Maxim's Experiments in Aerial Navigation* The Century, Vol. 49, January 1895.

McFarland, Marvin W. *The Papers of Wilbur and Orville Wright.* Salem, NH: Ayer Co., 1990.

McMahon, John R. *The Wright Brothers.* New York: Grosset & Dunlap, 1930.

Miller, Ivonette Wright. *Wright Reminiscences/* Dayton, Ohio: The Air Force Museum Foundtion, Inc. 1978.

Moolman, Valerie. *The Road to Kitty Hawk.* Alexandria, VA.: Time-Life Books, 1980.

Mumford, Lou. *Family claims historical accounts of first flight aren't 'Wright'.* South Bend, IN.: South Bend Tribune, Oct. 11, 1998.

O'Dwyer, Major William J. *The "Who Flew First" Debate*: Flight Journal.

Parramore, Thomas C. *Triumph at Kitty Hawk.* Raleigh, NC: Division of Archives and History, North Carolina Department of Cultural Resources, 1993.

Patton, Phil. *Made in USA.* New York: Penguin Books, 1992.

Powell, William S. editor *Dictionary of North Carolina Biography.* Chapel Hill, NC: UNC Press, 1986.

Renstrom, Arthur G. *Wilbur & Orville Wright: A Chronology Commemorating the Hundredth Anniversary of the Birth of Orville Wright.* Washington, D.C: Library of Congress, 1975.

Roseberry, C. R. *Glenn Curtiss*. Syracuse, NY: Syracuse University Press, 1972.

Scott, Phil. *The Pioneers of Flight*. Princeton, NJ: Princeton University Press, 1999.

_____ *The Shoulders of Giants*. Redding, MA: Addision-Wesley Publishing, 1995.

Stick, David *The Outer Banks of North Carolina*. Chapel Hill, NC: University of North Carolina Press, 1958.

_____ *Wright Memorial Museum Committee* (1959-1960) unpublished.

Sunderman, James F. *Early Air Pioneers*. New York: Franklin Watts, Inc., 1961.

Tipton, David A. and Stanley R. Mohler. *The Wright Brothers: A Personality Profile*: Aviation, Space and Environmental Medicine, June, 1983.

Wescott, Lynanne and Paula Degen. *Wind and Sand*. New York: Harry N. Abrams, Inc., 1983.

Wright, Milton. *Diaries 1857-1917* Dayton, Ohio: Wright State University Press, 1999.

Wright, Orville. *How We Invented the Airplane*. Mineola, NY: Dover Publications, 1988.

Zumwald, Teresa.. *For the Love of Dayton: Life in the Miami Valley 1796-1996*: Dayton, Ohio: Dayton Daily News, 1996.

Annual Report for the Secretary of State to the Governor of the State of Ohio, year ending November 15, 1894. Columbus, Ohio: The Westbote Co., 1895.

Montgomery County Historical Society. *History of Montgomery County, Ohio*. Dayton, Ohio: 1997.

Prospectus for Museum. Wright Memorial Museum Committee of the Kill Devil Hills Memorial Society, 1952.

Wright Brothers Official Map and Guide. Wright Brothers National Memorial, Kill Devil Hills, NC: National Park Service, GPO, 2000.

The Elizabeth City *Independent* and *Economist,* 1900-1910.